Optimistic Organizations

Optimistic Organizations

*How to Get, Grow and
Keep Positive Power in
Your Company*

Jean A. Hollands

SELECT BOOKS
Los Altos, California

FIRST EDITION

ISBN 0-9632556-3-0 12.95

Producer: WATT & COMPANY
            111 Main Street, Suite 3A
            Los Altos, CA 94022

Publisher: SELECT BOOKS
            a division of Select Communications, Inc.
            4410 El Camino Real, #111
            Los Altos, CA 94022

Optimistic Organizations

How to Get, Grow and Keep
Positive Power in Your Company

Dedication

*To Don Wuerflein, my husband, and to all my friends
and family! These are the people who 'clean up' after
my sky's-the-limit efforts. Don, in spite of it all, you
believe in my optimism—that makes you one, kiddo!*

Acknowledgments

Grateful acknowledgment to my associates—who are incredible!
Joan Blake, A j Kessler, Richard Spath—and sixteen more
counselors—all walk the exciting lines with me. They let me test,
re-test and hypothesize all over them.

Thank you to my family, my mother, Helene Deigan, with
her "I guess you'll do it anyway, Jean," attitude, and with her
abundant love and support; and thank you to my three sons, Glenn,
Tom and Todd, who roll their eyes back and still love me. And
my special, inspiring, collegial daughter, Laura Beth Hollands-
Steck, and my children's mates, Patty, Ana and Ron, and my
husband's marvelous daughter, Sandy Pounds, and his sons, and,
of course, Don Wuerflein, my honey and help-mate.

And I am grateful to my friends—Joan Craig, Monica Chism,
Carol Marks; my professional friends—Bethel Watt, Trudy
Duisenberg, Scott Neely, Arlen Burger; and my Board of Directors—the Nybergs, Cosgroves, Leudtkes; and all the other mentors in my life—those big, bold, audacious teddy-bear mentors!

Thank you, Dr. Martin Seligman, for your contribution
through *Learned Helplessness* and *Learned Optimism*. You were
my inspiration.

And thank you to the 'helpless people' who have turned
powerful right before my eyes—the clients, the organizations, the
'recovering wimps' and everyone who has proved that optimism
is easier!

Introduction

Years ago, when a vice president of a company brought me a book about learned helplessness by Dr. Martin Seligman, actually entitled *Helplessness: On Depression, Death and Development,* I fell in love. With Dr. Seligman, that is. His ideas about patterns which indelibly shove you in the direction of helplessness, were exciting to me. My client, charming, brilliant, highly positioned, decided, with the help of this new notion of learned helplessness, that he had been a victim of helplessness. He realized he had been programmed to:

▲ give up power
▲ lose power
▲ lose hope
▲ lose jobs

Nearly a decade later, I came upon *Learned Optimism.* I fell in love again. I've never met Dr. Seligman, but he belongs in Silicon Valley, where power among leaders is essential. Seligman believes that optimism is learned and can be adapted to your way of thinking, your behavior and your reflex actions. I do too.

The vice president eventually recognized the signs and signals of feeling helpless. Then I could help him and others to identify signs of power and hope. We do learn optimism. The road to health, by the way, is faster than the road to dysfunction. With the joy and rewards of positive interactions and styles that work, we hurry along into optimistic attitudes, and, of course, they compound the progress we make.

We learn to:

▲ keep power
▲ not to personalize misfortune
▲ take feedback as data, not demands
▲ reframe negative situations
▲ keep the faith!

Working with organizations for nearly 20 years, I have come to recognize the good ones and the bad ones. What's the difference? Excellent products, excellent leaders, the right moment in time? As I can determine, one quality presides in the good companies—optimism!

This is a simple book. I've just noted a lot of rules and reminders about how to think 'power' instead of impotency. I've done some name-dropping of my favorite people, and enjoyed doing it! I've used 'he' throughout—forgive me, women—but we know 'he' and 'she' are eternally interchangeable!

Sniveling CEOs complain and whine and beg to know why the people under them are not as enthusiastic or energetic as they are. "Inspire your people," I demand. "Acknowledge them in their form," I coach. "What is their form?" the CEO demands. "That's precisely why you are in trouble," I hiss.

I get so frustrated with complaining managers who don't believe or trust their own companies. "Fix yourself," I yell. "I can't be fixed," they scream back. Then I retort, "Neither can the company!"

I get so disappointed with employees who don't respect their managers. "Teach your bosses what you need in order to respect them," I insist. "They won't change," the employees cry. "You mean you won't hope," I groan. That means **change—that means be an optimist!**

Optimistic organizations are those companies, agencies, families, units of people which, in the total, believe in the best possible outcomes. They are sure that the best outcome is possible for the employees, the players and the individuals. They also believe that the best is possible for the organization as a whole. They live, breath, teach, preach hope!

Hope is the magical transcendation from despair and bleak outlooks to a tiny glimmer of a win, a yes, a profit, a reward. Hope is a miracle you can believe in. Without it, the faith that the company and your efforts will count for something, you are doomed to attach yourself to all the negative and pessimistic possibilities that are available to you.

Why is it so easy to give up hope? Our society grooms us well. We are graded at every turn. Failing is debilitating and causes death in many cases. Measurement tools—they surround us. We've got *profit and loss statements, quality assurance, venture capitalists,* the *accounting department* and the *stock market* and *insider trading* and the *board of directors,* the *police,* the *customers,* the *clients,* the *vendors.* We've also got history books to measure you. "It's never been done," they say.

So you have to believe you are special. Start to believe that your product is special, your team is, your efforts will be. Then you've got a chance—your only chance to be an optimistic organization!

Chapter 1

Optimistic Organizations: What Do They Look Like?

What Is Optimism?

The El Camino YMCA Mission Statement:

The YMCA is dedicated to strengthening and enriching the mental and physical and spiritual wellness of all people and to improving human conditions within the changing patterns of family and community life.

This mission statement above symbolizes optimism. The Y believes it can help. It wants to. And it believes that the changing society requires this help. When I walk in the door every morning, I see the motto, big, bold, hanging out of the sky light window, with light reflecting through it, and hope reflecting all around it.

Why do some organizations make it while others fail? Why do twin companies result in one winning and one losing? Why are venture capitalists often surprised? Why do teams with the perfect complementary players die? Since high profile leadership, abundance of capital, company SAT scores, exquisite products and good management skills do not insure successful organizations, what in the world does? When we look at companies, Olympic hockey teams, all sporting events, opera houses, international achievements, a sustaining quality prevails.

The sustaining quality appears to be hope. The organization is hopeful. There is joy at every stage of growth, from the organizational adolescence of chaos to the bureaucratic stage of rules and order. There is joy in the process from infancy to organizational maturity.

Optimism is a way of looking at life, your mate, your handicaps, your challenges. It is simply looking with positive glasses—not  rose colored, idealistic glasses—but with a positive eye. It is a belief that the journey is worth the effort.

These are worth it:

- ▲   the difficult employee
- ▲   the tyrannical boss
- ▲   the frustrating board
- ▲   the tumultuous highs and lows

This book is easy to read. There are no complex formulas or theories. Act positive, smile, walk happy, and you will feel better. Others will too. Your brain does not know the difference between practicing positive and actually, authentically, with cause, feeling it!

Optimism Is A Switch

You can turn it off or on. You have the choice. You can choose joy or hope, or you can choose despair and impotency.

In organizations, the circumstances do not matter. The company's response to circumstances matter. Your attitude matters. You can lose your biggest account and turn the company into another form—better, stronger and, if you wish, ultimately bigger.

If you lose your significant grant, your president, your sponsor, you can survive. Your prevailing attitude can make the difference. In the last five years, I have worked with three companies whose founding presidents have died prematurely. A 'we can do it' attitude guided each company through the tragic transition.

Optimism is a belief that things go wrong, ships sink, nuisances happen. Optimistic Organizations prepare, shake off the fear, move forward and cope. They do not act surprised at failure. They expect it. They expect it only *some of the time!*

Expect The Best, The Most, The Highest

Optimistic Organizations make it look easy. Their presidents make it look easy. Their staff and their policies look easy. Because they know it is easy.

Optimistic Organizations demand the **best**. Are you doing this? Expecting the best from your product, customers and staff? Be optimistic enough to know that a positive approach is also an informed approach, so an Optimistic Organization will always plan with realistic numbers in place. Safe numbers may be procured by the more pragmatic CFO who normally presents a conservative approach, based on 'worst case.' A presentation with Zest can clean up some sorry numbers.

The 'best case' is also always included.

Best case:

▲   opens up possibilities
▲   makes work satisfying
▲   promotes excitement
▲   stimulates hope
▲   incentivizes the project
▲   sets some people on fire

Everyone needs to believe his task, project, job is worthwhile. So Optimistic Organizations have a rationale for every task, project, product and strategy. They think ahead, anticipate what the guy in assembly, the stock holder, or the last chair in the secretarial pool will be thinking about this move. No major strategy is contemplated without some preventive thinking about what impact this has on the optimism of each member of the organization.

The Other Shoe Will Fall!

"I don't want to get too happy because something bad may happen," is pessimist talk. Don't worry about the other shoe falling. It will. In the meantime, you will be having a wonderful time enjoying the success you have.

Or, others say: "The fear of possible disaster pushes me to work hard. If I were not afraid to fail, I might get lazy." This is faulty logic. The anxiety can often be debilitating, not motivating. The terror of possible loss can be paralyzing. Try to be creative when you are tense with fear. It's not easy.

The problem with superstition is that you have programmed yourself not to get going unless you are scared or rushed. When you feel hurried or tense, your reflex action is to get into gear. Those programs can be very ingrained. For awhile, as you are giving up pessimism and helplessness, you will have to keep reminding yourself to work a little harder even when you don't feel the push of trauma or deadline.

Use whatever reinforcement method it takes—rubber bands, rewards, trainings, accountability prompters, sponsors, anything to get you motivated **except** drama or deadlines. In the early stages, you will not easily be motivated without the superstition of pessimism. As you discover the rewards of work without stress, of watching others struggle with their frenzied deadlines, you can relax with the knowledge that you have already finished the task. With this happy realization, you will begin to give up the destructive pattern.

Learn to be early, first, ahead of schedule. Plan small rewards for yourself for each completed task. Don't regret, worry over what more you could have done to enhance the work. Perfectionists are always procrastinators, because there is always one more piece of research which could have been applied.

Learn to applaud your incremental milestones. Without the perfectionistic tendency you can begin to praise yourself for the early steps accomplished. Try to relax as you work. Chant: "I can only do the best that I can do." As you complete each incremental chore toward the end result, be grateful for that. Learn to love your infinitesimal milestones.

As you give up perfectionism, you will also be giving up procrastination. Of course, you will also have to give up your procrastinators club—and its annual convention at the post office at midnight on April 15th!

Our company is paid a lot of money to teach employees to give up perfectionism. We know there are times when perfect results are expected, but unless you are an astronaut or brain surgeon, you can begin to give up the stress and debilitation of perfectionism.

Learned Helplessness

Dr. Martin Seligman did an experiment in 1965 which brought insight to the notion of helplessness. We do learn the feeling of helplessness and impotency. Then we recall that feeling when we are in situations which could remind us of the earlier helplessness.

Seligman created three groups of dogs in three situations:

- ▲ group one, which were placed in box with low barrier and no shocks
- ▲ group two, same box, but shocked until jumping over the barrier
- ▲ group three, same box, no cessation of shock under any circumstances

Then he later placed all three groups into yet another experiment, each group now having a low barrier over which they jump to stop the shocks. (Now, I own a dog, so please bear with me.) The dogs survived. But the dogs from the three groups reacted differently.

Group one and group two dogs jumped the barrier and stopped the shocks. Group three dogs remained on the shock side. They did not jump over the low barrier to stop the discomfort.

In this breakthrough test, he noted that the dogs in group three learned helplessness, and could not jump. They could not even try to jump.

Are humans like dogs? Yes and no. We have more complex brains, of course. Can we learn to jump over the barrier even when we earlier learned helpless experiences? Yes, we can. Do we? Sometimes, no.

Have you watched an executive freeze when he is faced with the chairman of the board who stripped him of his power at the last meeting?

Have you seen a woman, watch in terror, at the hospital door, if tragedy greeted her there previously?

Is there carry-over from one powerless situation to the next? Yes, there is memory carry over. Can you re-program yourself when the similar situation occurs? That is what this book is all about. You can. You can learn to.

Children who have never won a spelling bee or a foot race or a contest or even a raffle ticket are much less inclined to take a risk in other arenas.

Think about your areas of learned helplessness. Mine are singing (my second-grade school teacher told me I couldn't) and driving (I flunked my first several driving tests). What are yours? Are they about math, loving, organization, speaking in public, argument styles, violence fears, logic, athletics, your sensitivity?

We have handicaps. We can learn to overlay past experiences with new and better ones. This is the nature of optimism. One small success, one hit of the ball, once dance move, one small speech can begin to make the difference. Give yourself permission for fear and old wounds, and then start to imagine you solving the problem—singing the National Anthem, organizing your briefcase, winning the argument and feeling hopeful in the old 'spooky' places.

Life Is A Rough Draft

Keep the goal up front. Make plans around it. Talk about it. Talk to the team. Let them dream. Let them dream concretely too. What if—raises, vacations, stocks, baby-sitting, research grants, new challenges?

If the goal isn't tailored to each group or, hopefully, to each individual, you haven't a viable 'best.' What does Wanda, the executive secretary in Zephyr products, care if your company goal is to be the eighth largest in the world? Someone in the organization will care! Make sure that guy knows 'that' goal. Wanda may want the goal to be a six-week vacation for every employee.

Test the goals for a minute. Send someone on one of those trips, give someone time off. Experiment and don't be afraid to make correction adjustments. Life is a rough draft.

Asian restaurants are a good model for individualizing goals. Each person, with a different appetite, can choose a particular dish. Some of the dishes will be tasted by all, some by a few.

Plan for individualizing goals and rewards. Don't worry about the extra work. Teach members accountability—to tasks and to getting their needs met. Supervisors can help too. Those individualized goals should be just as important as performance reviews. Even though we may be ordering a variety of values, as though from a Chinese menu, there will be clusters of people who want the same goals. Some individuals are so unique that they need specialized goals.

If the organization you are with does not even have your goal on the menu, you may simply have to leave. Better yet, don't leave until you have tried your best to instill this value into your organization. Campaign for what you believe in. If the campaign fizzles, leave the organization. But, first, give it your best effort. Go round 2, 3, 4. . .

Jiggle The Adrenaline!

Everyone needs an adrenaline pump periodically. Make sure that announcements sound hopeful and **not like obituaries**. If you can't think of anything positive to say about your company, say something positive about the world, your chief engineer, the landscaping, someone's favorite charity.

Lighten up! A good adrenaline jump can be a bit of humor. Nothing sends the endorphins rushing like a good belly-laugh. Why do you suppose we have so many reproduced cartoons that swirl through organizations year after year. Some are raunchy, some are profound. All bring a giggle for some of you.

A deep laugh feels healthy. It can reduce tension, create good will, and free you to take a more realistic look at yourself and situations around you.

If you are not a humorist yourself, ask someone from your staff to help you to put out humorous or at least cheerful announcements. If you have no one on your staff who is funny, start recruiting.

You can learn a sense of humor. You can even

learn to be funny. Try watching or listening to funny people. It is not about remembering jokes!

Get your own organizational Will Rogers. You will learn a lot from him, but he will also become engaged in your problems. Keep that person close to you. For comfort. For reality checks. **Why was the court jester always so near the king?**

Try for the humorous approach when possible. Having that humorous person on your side will enhance the whole culture of your company. A 'Mash mentality' is necessary when overwhelming obstacles, without relief, are washing over your organization. Wanting a 'buy in' for your ideas often needs a multilevel sales pitch. When you can't be profound, try being silly. Try anything to make your point!

Don't Overwork Anyone

In rare and dire circumstances, every organization must ask for extra output. But don't let it become a company culture. Some companies attract that over-achieving martyr who seems to have nothing else to do anyway. These stress Type A behavior patterns are great in a crisis, they take the stairs, two at a time, and you will often find them alone on a Sunday afternoon—at work.

There is a big price to pay for the benefits of a Type A worker. The three Type A characteristics are: time urgency, competition, and hidden anger. Eventually the hidden anger makes an appearance—usually when you least expect or need it. The other cost of the over-achiever is that he will eventually burn out! In the middle of the audit or the board meeting or the final days of the software programming, the star will simply become strained and walk away.

Encourage balance. Encourage a life! Encourage social, spiritual, philanthropic, athletic, family endeavors. If you are sending someone out of town, make a point of acknowledging the family sacrifice and the special effort your employee is making. Make overtime the exception, not the rule.

If your special person has no friends or family, as is often the case, encourage support systems for him. Ask another employee to join him on the trip. Oh, I know. 'Hermit' would rather eat alone, go to shows alone, and doesn't even want to sit next to the 'chaperone' on the plane, but the notion that they are still traveling together is a help and will begin to plant the cooperative, team-building seed.

Now, you say, isn't that going a little too far for this individual contributor who does better alone anyway? Yes, sometimes it is. I am simply trying to help to raise your consciousness that the socially introverted player eventually will demonstrate the handicap of isolation and an inability to receive feedback.

In the late 1970s, I did a little research project on **Depression and Aloneness.** I asked people to enumerate the number of hours they spent alone, eating, driving, going to movies, being at home, taking breaks, and working alone.

Is it any surprise that the 700 subjects who spent the most of the time alone correlated with the 700 subjects who, by their own admission, felt the most depressed. I know people talk about the difference between 'alone' and 'loneliness.' My subjects did not report they were lonely. They were only asked how much time they spent alone.

If your CEO or any other influent spending the better part of their lives on persuasive agent and ask for a meeting eager-beaver CEO. Simply ask the pers like:

> *"Your employees are expecting you to set a good example by not putting every pore of your body into this company. We want you to survive this year. We want you balanced and alert and healthy, and we believe only you can set the standard for this."*

Now, if you are already rolling your eyes back in your head as you read this, bear with me. You have got to become an optimist too. You can believe that being an agent for positive change is worth the effort. I want you to imagine that you, alone, can make a difference.

Oh, it may take a second effort. Maybe the persuader can't do it alone. Or do it the first time. Or maybe he is not the right persuader. Maybe you will need to pick another agent; someone the CEO really respects and admires. If that person is also a workaholic, he can start the conversation out with, "You know, Jack. I've been thinking about you and me. I want us around for our company reunion in five years."

Or, "You know, Jack, people have complained to me that I look haggard and you look like you've eaten too many persimmons. Why don't we take a look at our image? What are we saying to our employees?"

⸛crets

Secrets kill. I know. Sometimes there are the 'safety of our world' secrets. Or there are audits or special circumstances where morale suffers with premature information. I'm talking about secrets in general.

Try to keep the strategic political moves of your organization in everyone's view. Don't delude, deny or distrust the emotional maturity of an employee who gets the facts. I've had too many people in my office who could say, "I know it is best for the company in the long run, and I'm glad they had the courage to do it."

Keep evaluations so public that promotions seem inevitable. I am not suggesting publishing annual reviews on the bulletin board. There are subtle ways of letting others know when someone has gone beyond the call. Memos commending good work and other public notification of high level work reveals to others those who are performing.

Don't reward workaholism. That employee will ultimately charge you with his stress compensation benefits. Or he won't wear well with others. Usually they just wear out.

If you promote someone, and it wouldn't make any sense to most people, say why. Tell your constituents that you are making a decision in your interest, or because of your own bias, or because he is your brother-in-law. If it is legal and ethical but just stupid, admit it. Say, "Bear with me, folks, on this one."

I have many executives in my practice who moved whole companies to Wyoming or England because they were Wyoming-o-philes or the other 'philes.' They admitted it was a prejudicial move, but they knew the company needed a happy and peaceful executive.

Don't try to rationalize the irrational. Tell the truth. Some will claim you are selfish; some will say you are sticking to your values and that you are modeling taking care of yourself. Some will say you know what you want to work for the company. When decision-makers take responsibilities for their own needs, workers under and around them don't have to take responsibility for them.

Secrets breed rumors. Rumors are usually much worse than the truth. A 'broken ankle' can turn into being 'carried off to the State Mental Hospital.' I know that's why we have seen every President's colon and prostate gland in living color.

Everybody Is In Sales

Teach everyone in your organization to sell himself, his ideas, projects, solutions and philosophy. Start with the janitorial service. Let them try to convince you that working at 6 a.m. is better for everyone than cleaning at midnight. Next, teach accountants to sell their red flags, to pronounce the numbers in ways you can hear them, and to market their company-saving procedures to other departments.

Coach that selling simply means the friendly art of persuasion. 'Sad sacks' who run out on their own—out of the meeting, out of the building, out of the organization—because nobody will adopt their ideas, usually haven't been able to describe or sell their ideas well.

A Fortune 500 called us in to sell some very sophisticated R&D engineers, right from MIT and Stanford, on the idea of persuasion as a skill needed at the top. It worked!

I gave a speech recently at IEEE, Denver, on **Persuasive Skills for Technical Professionals**. Do those skills help at home, with the dog, with your barber, on the dance floor, on the little league field? Absolutely.

When a very important GM/EDS executive asked me if my leadership training would help him with his teenager, I emphatically affirmed in the positive. Sure, he was a commander, a commando, a Vice President, a leader. His management of people was Great Santini-ish. He had never learned soft sell, reflective listening, addressing objections, and all the ways to get your point accepted in the long run. Selling needs to be tuned to the customer, your teenager, your colleagues.

The persuasive worker can sell deadlines to bosses or customers, limitations to technical projects, can sell one man on another and one concept to a room full of potential collaborators.

Optimistic Organizations are always selling the product, the mission, the employees, the management style, the way they do business, and hope.

Optimistic Organizations know themselves. They know their weaknesses and assets. They know very well what they can't do, or what they choose not to do. They could make all their own parts but realize it would not be cost effective. They know, love, and advertise their best traits—"nobody can do it faster, more efficiently, more sensitively, more conservatively," more flamboyantly.

Optimistic Teams don't procrastinate. Why should they have to? They are sure of the course, of course! If the course proves to be wrong, they admit it and start again. They are not afraid to make a mistake. They know mistakes are inevitable. They don't have to always get it right the first time.

The National Association of Women Business Owners (NAWBO) is an example of an optimistic organization. Margaret Smith, Los Altos attorney, founded this local chapter. Each woman business owner owns a very stable, growth-oriented company, but she also believes in working and giving to a bigger organization, NAWBO, in spite of the challenge of working with women who have made their own ways independently. Bobbie Fakkema, Events Etc., current Bay Area Chapter president, is an example of optimism. San Francisco 'Entrepreneur of the Year,' Bobbie presides with enthusiasm and vigor in spite of the 2% average with which women's businesses are used in governmental bids, and in spite of the energy required to compete with networks older and more political.

NAWBO takes on the challenge for women. Legislatively, financially, culturally, this organization will make a difference. Its motto is "Women Mean Business"— one of NAWBO's visions is:

> *"Managing the course of change, and changing the course of management."*

How To Sell Yourself, and Other 'Worthy' Causes!

David Markham knows his design will do the job. Harold wants the new man on his team. Sue wants a larger budget for her project. Bob Brown wants the raise he deserves. How do these people get

what they want? By selling their ideas and credentializing themselves! It is not enough to have the best design or the best record.
You also have to make the appropriate moves to sell yourself and
your project.

Some of you have learned to be humble about yourself and
your ideas. You were trained that boasting is sinful. I am not
talking about bragging. Some of you can sell your designs and
products better than you can sell yourself. Sales psychology is not
included in every college curriculum.

During an MIT, Minnesota, 50th anniversary conference,
where John Sculley of Apple Computer and I key-noted in 1990,
the Dean of Engineering declared they were considering a *"Selling Yourself"* course in the engineering curriculum. "I personally
missed out on a lot of work because I would not speak up,"
reminded another 1960 Nobel winner from that institution.

"I wonder why I was so shy in those days," commented
another noted authority in the electronics world. "I could have
gotten the work done faster if I had just insisted on a few things."

The sales game is not always made up of a selective process
determined by facts. Don't assume that logical facts will win the
sale. Psychologically speaking, people or organizations buy based
on intuition, impulse, feeling good about the product or the
persuader, as well as a calculating approach to rational conclusions.

Keys to Successful Selling:
Enthusiasm! Enthusiasm! Enthusiasm! If enthusiasm is not your
game, make some practice attempts to appear to be lively and
committed to the event at hand. Programming emotional vigor
is possible. Coaches do it before games. Sales managers do it at
sales conferences. Presidents do it at trade shows. You can do it

for yourself—by self talk and acting 'as if.' Even when it is not your natural stance, try it for short periods. Tell yourself that you are doing this for a cause greater than you, and allow yourself to feel stupid, silly or out of character, **because** you want the final result.

People new at selling their ideas or projects often give up after the first try. Don't let this happen to you. Learn basic sales techniques: Every 'no' is on the way to a 'yes.' If you aren't getting any 'no's' you may not be stretching your boundaries enough. Every 'no' is a possible 'maybe.' Every 'maybe' is a possible 'yes.'

Use Words That Sell!

Give up on equivocating words or phrases like "I can't think of any reason why not," or "I guess" or "probably."

Try stronger and more promising phrases like: "This may determine the future of your business." Or, "We strive for excellence." Or, " A luxury that is within your reach."

Tell the other person that you want to work together, that you like the idea of the two of you making a project happen, that you are excited about him, her, the concept.

Use words that sell:

- ▲ high
- ▲ up
- ▲ promise
- ▲ want
- ▲ can
- ▲ pride
- ▲ stride
- ▲ excellent

Don't use:

- ▲ maybe
- ▲ probably
- ▲ sometimes
- ▲ almost
- ▲ think
- ▲ if
- ▲ wish

Excited? No, that may not be a word you would use. 'Excited' you are not! Then find a word that fits and one that also sells. The phrase "This project interests me very much," is not as good as "I am the man or the woman for this task. I can do it!"

Phases of Selling Yourself:

The Planning Phase is the most important work you can do. It is the strategic and visionary time in which you develop your strategy and sales technology to sell the idea. This is the idea generation time, when your project development has to be innovative and well thought out. The goal is just to get someone's attention or ear.

Pessimists are afraid to plan. They are afraid they will seem too grandiose, the project will be too overwhelming or silly. They are afraid to take a chance. Do it. Do it for exercise. Don't worry about humiliation. Worry about the stagnant life of never risking.

In the **Sales Innovation Phase,** you want your ideas to ring out, count, and energize those who must take it to the next step. Optimism allows you to be more creative and gives you an opportunity to evaluate your product as different and essential. Talk about why you or your idea or your product is so indispensably unique!

In the **Priorities Phase,** you make sure that you and your prospect both think that talking with you is important—that you have something that fits into his agenda needs. If you or your product are not on his priority list, you can begin to teach him why you need to be! Always look for the influence niche, the need, the way in to the emotional door of the possible customer or client or colleague.

In the **Promotion Phase,** you do the work you usually think of as sales. This is when you make the call, follow up, give feedback, raise your image, highlight the benefits, and then call again, follow up, give feedback, raise your image, highlight the benefits, and then call again, follow up, give feedback.

In your political life in an organization, the calls are more elusive and subtle. Sometimes it is just a memo, a visit at the copy machine, a word or two with the president—any gesture that follows up the theme you are wishing to extend.

Be Flexible!
Trust you will get the job, the promotion, the grant, the materials. Sometimes this takes a minor shift in directions, a delay, a detour or someone else looking over your shoulder. Take five steps back, try to look at your ideas from the other point of view. For a moment, live in his shoes, dig in to his values, his thinking process and decision-making style. Sales people are even taught NLP (Neurolinguistic Programming). Is he a visual, auditory or kinesthetic person? Charts or oral presentations or a good 'hands on' experience? Sell to your receiver, not to you, the sender!

Working Your Supporters, Not Your Detractors!

When you need to make a sale of yourself or your service or product, make sure you recognize your own support system. Your support system can be made up of four categories of C's:

C: **Comfort:** Just plain old nurturing support: "You've got the stuff, John."

C: **Clarification:** "Let me help you to replay the scenario again, Ruth. First, you—then, he."

C: **Cultivation:** This supporter actually helps you put a plan in place. "I'll call my Venture Capitalist friend for you, Harry."

C: **Confrontation:** This supporter will give you a kick just where you need it. "C'mon, Mark, stand up and make the move!"

Of course, other compadres will want to look for flaws in your theory and design, but watch out for the person who simply wants to prove you wrong to get his own attention! Facing the rational and technical aspects of your design or project is the least of your concerns. So spend a little time on the 'other side' of the sale— the psychology of the customer!

Don't Press, Impress!

While I urge perseverance, don't try to 'stuff' the material down someone's throat. Instead, impress him with your desire to do the job, with your skill and commitment, and your abilities and background. Your product is important because you think it is. You are important because you know you are! Now convince someone else. It is worth the task. Selling may be the hardest skill you will ever acquire. And the one that buys you the most opportunity.

An optimist loves to sell anything. You will love the challenge, the opportunity to show your assets, and you will be rewarded with the emotional high that someone 'buys' your idea, your project, or you!

Chapter 2

Why We Need New Corporate Cultures

I am writing this book in the middle of the worst recession that Silicon Valley has had in decades. Not only are we facing unemployment, we've had a five year drought, the Santa Cruz landslides, the San Francisco earthquake, and the Oakland Hills fire, lately. We even had the Bay Area freeze which last year killed more outdoor landscaping than any bug, breeze or act of nature has in a century.

By the time this book is published, by the way, the recession may be ending and it will probably be raining cats and dogs here. (This proves I'm an Optimist.)

My point is that things change. Silicon Valley, the golden nugget of the world ten years ago, is having a rough spell. So we need the kind of organizational attitude that helps societies through the famine and the drought. We need the upbeat, 'we can do it' mentality. Organizations don't need the fair weather players who can be brave and do a lot of whistling when things are great anyway.

Organizations need optimists who will whistle in the downsizing, when the grant gets turned down, the major company stops the sale, the board members rebel, or the production halts.

Organizations need their our own form of Winston Churchill, who could rally the masses, soothe those in the black-out shelters and steady those running under the wind of the bombers.

Since we are democratic and very individualistic by nature, no one person can save our corporate morale. Each organization needs its own morale-booster. You may need special, individualized, customized type of a cheerleader who will help you through your own organizational and personal crisis. By the way, those cheerleaders don't have to carry pom-poms or deliver in bumptious ways. They don't need the passion of Tom Peters. They don't need the vision of Tom Jefferson. They just need to be believable, not grandiose. But they must demonstrate trust in the cause, the players, the structure.

If You Are All Through Changing. . .

If you are all through changing, you are all through! We are in a period, worldwide, where the USA, USSR, China, the rest of the world, is passing from one developmental stage to another. How quickly we've adapted to visual phones, pen based computers, clocks in our calculators and calculators in our clocks. How quickly we adjust to obsolescence. Yet we want to endure. We want the quality of our lives to be growing and glowing. We beg, "Please, don't obsolete me."

I heard Delaine Eastin, our local Assemblywoman, speak recently. She reminded us that in times of chaos we as a country still get things done. Times have been changing since the beginning of history. Delaine reminded us that in the dreadful crisis after the Civil War, we established public school systems. After the Great Depression, the bay area built The Golden Gate Bridge and the Bay Bridge.

My 81 year old mother looks in awe at computers and video tapes and electronic kitchens. Recently, she sighed and looked sadly at the electronic typewriter my husband bought me to start my first book. It is dusty, tucked on the floor in the corner—my formerly shiny, bright blue IBM Selectric! Within 12 years it has become our family dinosaur..

And the irony is that I had a portable Royal typewriter for 30 years before that. It got me through college, through my kid's college, and now my shiny Selectric is buried, without ceremony, in the corner, next to old love letters, battered dictionaries, and toys the puppy drags in. Times change.

Don't stop the change. You can't. Look with anticipation at the possibilities ahead of you—of the world. The optimist knows there are surprises in store for you.

People Want To Feel More Powerful

We won't all walk on coals to feel more powerful. But we are learning to like ourselves. We teach self esteem in movies, kindergarten, graduate school, and in corporate America. We believe that liking ourselves helps. So we want to feel that power in an organization too. We want to give it to subordinates, and the most evolved of us even want to give it to our bosses. Optimistic Organizations thrive on creating places and purposes for powerful people. The nature of optimism is that there is enough for all. Enough opportunity, decisions, goods and good will for all.

So with the masses asking more questions, the organization must have more answers. You can even decide to anticipate more of the answers. With the media so available to us, the doubting viewer can question more readily.

Company newsletters even encourage probing concerns and a democratic worry over corporate policies. Information is so readily available that no one can make a decision without analysis from one side or the other. It's hard to take a stand, or take the stand, these days. Your remarks will echo around the video world. Optimistic Organizations are aware of the instant feedback syndrome and are prepared for having to have a much thicker hide than that of the Honeywells and Westinghouses and Carnations of yesteryear.

Powerful women are beginning to change the world. My AAUW (American Association of University Women) friends, Vickie Reeder and Cecelia Keehan, are women who re-entered the corporate world with vigor. They say what they mean, state convictions boldly, but also take feedback. AAUW is an example of an optimistic organization.

People Want Balanced Lives Now

We are out of the era of work, the satisfaction of blind ambition, and production as a sign of worth. We are into an era of holistic balance. That means you can work a little, play a little, and have the whole world! That's the meaning of life. Wow!

The Reverend John Dodson and the Los Altos Methodist Church are examples of courageous and innovative institutions. John, an institution himself, radiates hope and energy.

Another positive friend of mine, Paul Nyberg, and his wife, Liz, grew *Select Communications,* publisher of seven magazines, with love and enduring faith in their staff and products.

The Mountain View Chamber of Commerce, with Executive Director, Barbara White, Leadership Chair, Mary Kate Franci, and Mayor Art Takahara, all demonstrate positive, 'we can do it' thinking who believe in the City of Mountain View, California, and potential for leadership within.

If your association is thinking positively, it will want you to feel balanced, to come to the organization full to the top from wherever you have been, and ready to support, supply and demand whatever you need from your organization.

This may be:

▲   Day care centers
▲   Parental leave
▲   Family caregivers leave
▲   AA meetings at work
▲   Fitness centers
▲   Impaired doctors meetings
▲   Impaired nurses, attorneys meetings
▲   Distinguished Employee Programs
▲   Sensitivity for managers
▲   Assertiveness for supervisors training

These classes or services are being offered in many of the progressive companies. Hewlett Packard has led the way in balancing employee needs with employer needs. Smaller companies are thinking wellness for their employees. Some companies supply fresh orange juice daily for their people. Some provide trips to Disneyland. Others simply provide confidence.

Times have changed. The salt mines are dry. Empty. We can't, won't, work the way we used to work. The twenties and thirties are over. And the eighties are over too.

The Dual Career, Dual BMW Days Are Over For Now

People crave the simpler life, the smaller house, and they are willing to make the financial sacrifices to stay at home with the kids, or to be a recycler, or to do whatever their values pull them toward.

We have to do work in more fruitful ways, so that when your eight or ten hours is done, you have energy for more than reading the paper, watching the news and dropping into bed. Optimistic Organizations encourage, praise, promote employees for all the efforts beyond the current work day. These groups talk, write, reward balanced lives. It is a fine line they walk; to get the job done, and get a worker who will get the job done. I'm not saying its easy.

The Myth of the Over-Achiever

The Old World over-achieving 'super employee' does not become the enduring employee the business world of today demands. Do you, or does anyone you know, exhibit the following character-istics on the job, and probably in your personal lives too?

▲   Always busy and in a hurry. Moves, sometimes fran-tically, from one event to the next. Schedules a full calendar for day and evening. Makes detailed schedules for weekends or leisure activities. Gets to work before most others, leaves later, and usually takes work home.

▲   Works at several things at one time, such as: making many calls on the car phone while driving between appointments; making notes about business activities during church or at a concert; holding side conversations or dictating letters while talking on the phone; reading the newspaper, making notes or eating dinner while watching TV.

▲   Speaks rapidly and forcefully, or finishes sentences for others, to keep conversations moving. Taps fingers or feet or makes other repetitive gestures during meetings.

▲   Takes on all offered assignments, especially those with extremely tight deadlines, and expects others to do likewise.

▲   Acts impatiently or discourteously with others who move less quickly or who perform tasks differently. In some environments, such an energetic and hard-driving individual is considered to be an ideal employee who gives 110% and is willing to undertake difficult tasks on extremely tight deadlines without complaint.

Some top organizational leaders long for a collection of such people who will make their wildest company dreams come true. Other leaders see such individuals as reflections of themselves, interpreting the employee's behaviors as containing the same dedication, loyalty and drive as he feels about his work and his company.

Do individuals with these behaviors actually exist? They do! Are such individuals good for themselves and the company? Definitely not!

We all realize that hard work and occasional long hours, balanced by other activities and interests, need not be harmful. However, the inner tensions and fears which cause these observed behaviors are known to be unhealthy.

What Does This Behavior Mean and Why Is It Unhealthy?

If you know someone with the behaviors we described, why would that be considered to be unhealthy? A considerable body of research has been developed on the Type A behavior patterns, founded by Dr. Meyer Friedman of San Francisco. This behavior has been described by Dr. Friedman as a more or less continuous struggle to do more and more in less and less time, usually against the opposing efforts of others. Doesn't that sound like the performance of an upwardly mobile overachiever?

The over-stressed Type A's exhibit typical vocal signs, such as:

- ▲ rapid, unevenly paced speech with the running-together or omission of final words
- ▲ clicking the tongue against the front teeth during normal speech
- ▲ clearly audible intakes of breath during speaking
- ▲ explosive, staccato, loud and frequently unpleasant sounding voice
- ▲ a hostile or jarring laugh; interrupts or hurries others
- ▲ uses obscenity in ordinary conversation; and fills speech with numbers and quantitative data

Also evident in our high stress organization man we'll find nonverbal behaviors like:

- ▲ tense posture, head-nodding while speaking
- ▲ repetitive and jerky hand, arm or leg movements
- ▲ hostile, confrontive responses to challenges
- ▲ makes angry generalizations about people
- ▲ is usually distrustful of people's motives
- ▲ exhibits anger when recalling past upsetting events
- ▲ makes a fetish of being punctual
- ▲ is never on time
- ▲ becomes irritable when required to wait or slow down
- ▲ performs several activities simultaneously
- ▲ may be competitive with children and plays games with adults only to win

The consequences of this behavior which was once revered and admired? Premature death from coronary heart disease or from the persistent practice of such self-destructive patterns as overeating, heavy drinking, failure to exercise, and a forced-draft working schedule involving as many as 20 hours a day, month after month. By attempting to do more and more in less and less time, this over-worked employee eventually reaches the point where intense activity takes the place of quality and meaningful productivity. Burn-out, serious errors in judgment, 'fire-fighting' activities with no long-range goals also result and will cause significant negative impact on employee performances, team morale and company profits.

Jeff Lugerner, GLC's sports and performance expert, and a member of the Meyer-Friedman Institute, recognizes that stress affects all aspects of performance and team reliability.

For more than 30 years, Dr. Friedman and his institute have been studying causes of coronary heart disease. His extensive research uncovered the fact that most coronary patients exhibit the behavior characteristics described. It has been found also that randomly selected persons exhibiting this behavior, whether male or female, are **seven times more likely** to have coronary heart disease as healthy persons not exhibiting this behavior, and they tend to have higher blood cholesterol levels and faster-clotting blood. Are you willing to take these risks for yourself, an employee, or your organization?

What Is A Healthy Employee?

As contrasted with the old stressed prototype, a Type B or innovative person of the 90s exhibits virtually none of the time-pressured and hostile behavior. The less stressed employee will provide long-term, quality results, on a dependable basis, while exercising good judgment and leading a balanced individual life style. This employee takes the time to make good decisions, produces consistently and, finally, generates more profit for the company.

Dick Spath, the CEO of our company, and my colleague in studying stress and the overachieving employee, has greatly assisted me in concentrating on the judgment that a non-stressed employee can demonstrate. The loss of the good judgment in critical moments by an overachiever can cost an organization dearly!

The over-stressed managers or leaders, when they do delegate, do so with trepidation and an air of irritability and impatience. Only if the delegee approaches the task in the same manner and at the same speed as he would, does he allow the task to be continued without interference.

The pressures of the high-paced, high-tech Silicon Valley environment encourages Type A behavior which, in turn, promotes a dramatically increased risk of premature death. It becomes important, then, to be able to identify the behavior of the over-stressed employee in individuals at all levels of the organization, and to help those individuals to learn appropriate new and healthy behaviors. When they do so, you will find them and your organization performing more smoothly with fewer resource-consuming crises.

How Do You Get To Be That 1990 Flexible, Innovative Employee of the 90s?

It is easier to teach yourself to be free-flowing and relaxed than it is to maintain the tight and rigid approach to getting everything done right and precisely on time.

Try holding out your arm and then clench-
ing your fist so tightly that your fingernails
begin to poke into the palm of your hand.
Then feel the muscle pull. It is difficult to do your best work, to be
creative, to work with ease when
the tension is pulling at your
muscles, whether brain
muscle or brawn muscle.

Plan on 'one minute vacations' to let yourself have the
reverie of a quiet and peaceful place washing over you for a
moment or two. Give yourself the acceptance during that moment—acceptance that you are doing the best that you can be
doing. The judgmental 'yes, but,' is the killer. "Yes, but I could
be working harder, smarter, longer, with more concentration," are
the critical voices which actually destroy creativity.

**Being compulsive and over-checking is, actually at the
extreme, a form of mental illness.** The stumbling blocks to
change are that you will feel 'itchy' and a little strange practicing
new behavior which is foreign to you. If you decide to resist being
first for a change, or you forsake your fifth check at your
document, you may be feeling a little insecure about yourself.

Do you wear well in an organization? Are others around
you, who in the beginning seemed so enthusiastic and creative,
starting to slow down and dip into dark and weary moods? How
do you know you are finally a Type B or an enduring employee?

The stressed Type A people are exciting and usually involved
in crisis moments in a company or a project, but their long term
usefulness and objectivity is often at a stake. Look for employees
and for yourself to exhibit the longevity of enduring predictabil-

ity, limit-setting and assertiveness. Watch for the employee who is always on the run, always harried and never seems to breathe! He, she, **you,** can be dangerous to an organization.

Relapses and detours happen. Allow yourself some slips back into the rigid and compulsive behavior during peak periods of stress. Getting down on yourself because you have, by reflex, turned anxious can only add to the tension. Take a deep breath and start your life again. It is your life, you know. Behind every audit, board meeting, presentation, confrontation or sales call— sits **your life!**

Test for 1990s Optimistic Members of The Organization

Always	5
Frequently	4
Sometimes	3
Rarely	2
Never	1

Enter: #5–1

1. There is not enough time for everything.   ____
2. I am a perfectionist about most things.   ____
3. I resist change in work structure.   ____
4. I am quite self-critical when things go wrong.   ____
5. I can feel overwhelmingly exhausted.   ____
6. I worry about ridicule.   ____
7. My work load is always bigger than I am.   ____
8. I take my work home with me in some form.   ____

9. I miss opportunities by not responding quickly.   ____

10. I don't celebrate my successes easily.   ____

11. There are too many deadlines in my life.   ____

12. Winning in most things is important.   ____

13. My anger surprises me.   ____

14. I'm known as a worrier.   ____

15. I'm called meticulous to a fault.   ____

16. I re-check myself, the doors-lights-stove, my work.   ____

17. Unexpected reactions disturb me.   ____

18. Surprises bother me.   ____

19. I put things off because I don't have everything ready. ____

20. I want to know the structure and agenda.   ____

21. Time is my enemy.   ____

22. I like to know what the possible outcomes are.   ____

23. I feel competitive.   ____

24. Disorder makes me feel tense.   ____

25. I am very hard on myself.   ____

26. I am victimized by current pressures.   ____

27. I enjoy routine.   ____

28. Shifting gears is hard on me.   ____

29. Too many choices concerns me.   ____

30. Polarized viewpoints bother me.   ____

31. I like to categorize.   ____

32. Too many approaches confuse me.   ____

33. I like working with my working style people.   ____

34. I hate to stop in the middle of a project.   ____

35. Ambiguous situations bother me.   ____

36. Things go wrong.   ____

37. I'm not important.   ——
38. Our organization is deteriorating.   ——
39. Hope is scarce.   ——
40. My colleagues could be better.   ——

——

Total each column and multiply by value of each   ——

The Innovative 1990s Executive Interpretation

40 to 60	You are flexible enough to work in a major position in the 90s. Decision-making is your forte and you are an asset to a brain-storming session.
61 to 70	An Enduring employee who will be an advantage to any organization. What a prize!
71 to 80	You can risk: cope with change well.
81 to 90	Adequately relaxed and flexible.
91 to 100	You can tend to get a little uncomfortable with change. You may be showing some signs of rigidity.
101 to 110	Exhibiting stress signs and seem to be a little too tense for your current situation.
111 to 120	Beginning to dread change and show some rigid and immobile characteristics.
121 to 130	Power loss evident.

<u>131 to 140</u>   You will be hard on a team because you compulsively resist stressful or ambiguous situations.

<u>141 to 170</u>   Your pessimism is showing.

<u>171 to 200</u>   Call for first aid!

The new culture for organizations is much more complicated than the old one. We have many more options for working than our parents did. Now we have choices about hours, benefits, individual contributor track or management track, being an entrepreneur or an intrepreneur, or being Mr. Mom or Mrs. Mom at home.

School kids have many more choices now. Even not going to college is an option now. With so many options, the individual is called upon to be self reliant and to manage his life based on individual values and not on family mores or social pressures. The individual is asked to take on a great deal more responsibility for his actions because his environment no longer dictates his destiny.

Our future was once dictated by the family we were born in. Later our sex, our location of birth, our birth order determined our destiny. Other determinants over history have been our race and our mental or physical prowess. Of course the mores of our culture played a part in our decisions too.

Now, however, a self-managed individual is not limited by the circumstances above. The helpless martyr, though, tries to use the excuses above not to manage his own life.

I'm not suggesting that there are not inequities still. I am only proposing that we have fewer inherent handicaps or structures which may determine our choices in life. We have learned that optimists do self manage and can make decisions based on their own needs and not just on acceptance or expectations from institutions or others.

This independence makes it difficult for organizations to practice authoritarianism. Individual differences pepper the differing management styles. Teachers have now learned that children learn in different ways, based on their temperaments, learning abilities, neurolinguistic programming, and their bio-chemical clocks. If teachers can teach twenty five kids who probably have eighteen different learning styles, we can learn to manage differences in working styles in organizations.

Of course, all organizations are not completely progressive. Teach your company. The bottom line is that with motivation theory in place, nearly every member or teammate or player or employee will march to a drum which he feels is especially designed for him.

Don't groan. The patterns do not have to be customized for each person. 15% will be motivated by one thing, another 35% by another, and 20% by specific and individualized programs. What about the last 30%? They will motivate themselves. They learned to get what they want before they joined your organization. They are the gems who seem to know how to play the game, pass the ball, go for the win, and smile all the way to the locker room.

Chapter 3

The Optimistic Leader

Looks, Feels, Sounds, Tastes, Presides Optimistically

If you have the privilege of running the show for now, first of all—enjoy it. It's actually much easier to make decisions and have an opportunity to delegate around them than to take orders from others. On the other hand, if you are the person who assumes too much responsibility, wants to please everyone every time, then I am sure the job is taking its toll on you.

But, let's assume you are a leader who knows just how much responsibility to assume and your only job in this chapter is to figure out if you are displaying enough good humor and optimism. Are you the model of the ideal optimist who walks like he talks?

I've heard hundreds of stories about the dedicated company leader who spends every waking moment at the company, or wakes in the middle of the night to prepare a memo for the next day, or who shows so much passion for the company or the product that nobody else seems to have to show much enthusiasm—the company leader does it for everyone.

But, let's assume that you are perfect in your balance between company and your other life, and all you need to do is test your ability to demonstrate the upbeat approach to things.

In the title of this chapter, I suggested that you look, sound and smell like an optimist. That means you seem present, appear interested, smile appropriately, wear positive, attractive clothes that will draw people to you. Each of you has your own style, whether its your management style or your own color palette (and many CEO's have had their 'colors done') but I'm only talking about what feels best for you and at the same time seduces people into wanting to believe you or be near you.

Sociological studies that indicate that people who are healthy looking and attractive:

- ▲ make more money
- ▲ cure more people
- ▲ sell more
- ▲ get more promotions
- ▲ are better paid
- ▲ marry better
- ▲ have fewer illnesses

In my profession, counselors who are well groomed and attractive seem to make more headway with clients than those who don't seem to care about how they present themselves.

Don't go out now and get your make-over. Just take in the notion that appearance may have some bearing on your progress.

If you have an overwhelming image of the commander, one who looks imposing because you are so big or your voice is so loud, you may want to overlay some complimentary appearance hints to tone down the look. Wear softer colors, walk more slowly, don't interrupt, and lighten your voice when you remember.

In my practice, I have a math teacher who works in a correctional school for very difficult boys. The teacher has a very pink face, a thin head of blondish gray hair and a narrow little voice. He actually appears to have a pre-set frightened look on his face. What can he do to tighten up his look a little? To command more respect, I asked him to stop wearing pink shirts, to wear epaulet shoulders on bold plaid shirts, to deepen his voice a little, walk with more deliberation, and practice the stern look instead of the scared one.

Now, To Look and Sound Optimistic, Remember To Believe That:

- ▲ the glass is half full
- ▲ people want to please you
- ▲ you are a good leader
- ▲ people can respect you
- ▲ you are capable of the tasks at hand
- ▲ it's just a matter of time

Talk in the present. 'If only' we had, and 'what if' are two 'ifs' which are too 'iffy' for your optimistic personality. Concentrate on today. If the past was awful, you can declare what you have learned, and congratulate yourself that the price of the mistakes has not killed you or the organization. Organizational disease may be close, you may be in Chapter 11 or beyond, but you need to talk like you got out of the jam just in time, and that you are grateful for the information.

The 'what if' is always forecasting doom. Stay in the present. Reframe your talk to be: "We are prepared for the inevitable. If situations arise, we can handle them because we are facing the future right this moment."

Chooses Optimistic Managers and Peers

When you have a chance to choose those who work for, around, or above you, choose those who say **why they can,** and drop those who say **why they can't.** Learn to listen to the worrier who starts out with, "Well, I've never done this before." It's okay that he admits the task is new, but look for the optimistic person who starts out with, "Well, this is going to be a challenge. I'll do my best. I've never done it before, but I'm eager to get started."

Listen for people who complained about the last job, boss, situation. Listen for patterns. Ask about successful times for him. Even if it was in high school, or winning the boy scout award, you want to know that he or she has felt success. If they hesitate too long, watch out. Now, some people are plagued by learned modesty and are reluctant to boast. You will have to screen through those folks and then listen for hints of success.

I always ask the question, "What will we eventually come to know about you that others have complained about before?"

This slows some down. You are looking for the person who can admit to some failing, but appears to be conquering it. "I've been told I'm too opinionated, but I'm learning to show more acceptance, to lower my stated expectations some. To compensate, I make opportunities to show my own vulnerabilities and shortcomings." What a turn-around set of statements!

Choose vice presidents to help you out. A Taylor Scanlon or a Mike Olson, two local vice president superstars, make their senior officers look good.

Presides Optimistically

Show enthusiasm. Reward an approximation of success. "John, we were close to the sales forecast this month. I'll bet you will make it next month."

When someone comes close to what you want, reward it. "Martha, you actually knocked this time when you interrupted us. I think you will even be more considerate next time. Thank you."

When we think of Ioccoca, do we remember how low his company was, how much in debt, and how near they were to disaster? No. We think of his enthusiasm, his strength to turn things around, and his bold and audacious suggestion for financial assistance.

When we think of Mikhail Gorbachev, do we think of the leader whose country was in desperate straights, with unrest in his troops and distrust all around him? No. We think of the smiling, waving man who seemed to radiate interest in change. What a leader! What luck for a country, actually for the whole world!

We have our own local heroes who have had different management styles, but who inspire enthusiasm from others: Ed Zschau, President of Censtor, Jerry Sanders from AMD, or Andy Grove from Intel. These men have weathered many business storms and always show the confidence and industry of a successful company CEO. Our female models for leadership hardiness are: Dr. Sharon Bray, Senior Vice President, General Manager, Lee Hecht Harrison; Dianne McKenna, Santa Clara Board of Supervisors; Susanne Wilson, CEO, Solutions By Wilson and former Santa Clara County Supervisor; and the consummate female CEO, Sandra Kurtzig, from our neighbor, Ask Computers.

Remembers The Big Pictures

You can't expect your staff to keep the long run in mind when the short run is grim. "I think, in the big picture, this organization is making headway. Now, the controller's numbers don't show it, but I've had calls monitored, and the meeting with the client went very well yesterday, so I believe we are on the right side of the mountain."

There is always a 'snagger' in every group. "Yes, but, boss, you said last quarter that we had to make it this quarter." Instead of letting you take care of the situation, he is pointing out a painful inconsistency. These 'snaggers' do it to get attention focused on them; not for the good will of the organization.

The Bigger Your Job, the Thicker Your Skin Should Be

Don't let those who enjoy getting you, get you! The higher your profile, the more opportunities people have to judge you. Allow that the increase in exposure is always an increase in opportunity to discredit you. Take it as part of the package; the price of your big responsibility, the price for being able to make decisions.

The optimistic manager is always looking for someone doing something right. Blaming, "Let's get to the bottom of this" folks simply stirs the fear and presents the negative instead of, "Next time I bet you'll all get this right." When you look to blame, you are inviting defensive attitudes. Someone has to be wrong, more at fault than others, and the opportunity for problem-solving decreases with the rising tension about being 'wrong.'

Re-Frames Crisis Situations

Being in charge offers you the opportunity to be informed when something goes wrong. Act as if you expect something will go wrong. Then prepare you and your staff to handle it. The optimistic doctor who has not had a malpractice suit simply expects that one day his number will be up, and he will be called to court. He does not frantically worry that every patient is a possible liability for him.

Your exterior needs to be calm. Remember Winston Churchill. His voice was strong and steady and he insisted that his country would survive—no, fight the bitter enemy as necessary, and win. Your exterior may need to find humor in the stickiest situation. Finding something light or funny about the situation, or better yet, about you, is relief-giving.

When President Bush vomited on the Japanese dignitary, he was quick to respond with how dramatically he 'can do the flu.' His wife, when discovering he was out of danger, quipped, "He's just mad because he lost in tennis this afternoon."

Finds The Rainbow

Find a rainbow in every possible storm. Sometimes the rainbow is late, hidden behind the clouds or the mountains or the buildings, but the belief that it is imminent, is vital. If you really want to be an optimist, you can trust that the pot of gold is out there too somewhere. Test your audience or your group. If you tend to be a little too flowery

or grandiose, relax with the pot of gold. Just keep that for yourself. The gold, that is.

Let's talk some more about rainbows. Your parents either believed in them or they didn't. If they did, and they were unrealistic dreamers, always hoping, without putting in the work to get the job done, you may have become disillusioned about rainbows.

Or you may have grown up with victims. Good things happened to other people. Bad things happened to your people. Your victim heritage can be overcome. Look back at your family history; you will probably discover that pessimism is a trait handed down from generation to generation. Well, stop the chain now. It is destructive, wasteful and boring.

If you had parents, or colleagues, or other influential people in your life who believed in rainbows, you will probably be looking for your own. A rainbow is a wonderful symbol for the terror of a thunder or rain storm and the peace of sun shining down all over the storm sites. A rainbow is like the results in your organization. You can endure chaos, thundering jolts, lightening strikes, hail-like people or situations, and then you can expect calm, warmth, understanding, hope, in the form of a sunny approach to the problems. Search desperately for that rainbow.

Assumes and Coaches Appropriate Responsibility

Teach the people who work around, or for, or above you, that we each have a limited arena of time and resources available, and that we cannot do more than is humanly possible. Lots of optimists are so much fun to work around, and their mission is so seductive, that the over-achiever is likely to be your worker-bee, and you need to keep that person monitoring himself.

"Let me know when you are feeling overwhelmed, Bill. This stuff gets to you after awhile."

Or, "Susan, I tend to push people to the wall. I want you here a long time, and I don't want you to burn out on me. So watch how much I pour on you, and yell 'uncle' when you need to."

Responsibility is a privilege. You can work with it, snivel, avoid, or shrink from it. Or you can enjoy the rewards of being a decision-maker, one who will assume obligation and accountability for others—and like it!

Believes in Self and Self-Directed Activities

If you are wanting others to follow you or cooperate with you, believe in your own goals. If you are feeling doubts and can't pull it off, go see someone who will give you a confidence boost. I have my own special pals who will pump me up when I've been stupid or someone has hurt my feelings. I can't always do it alone. Sometimes I just need someone else to say, "Well, they could be wrong, you know."

So, after the booster shot, come in with your best face, best hope and the words around it. Try these:

▲ "This is worth it."
▲ "We're on the right track."
▲ "We're just around the corner."
▲ "Given the obstacles. . . ."

Speaking of Givens, Try This On Yourself

Given the Givens: "Given who my mother was, or my father was, or my parent role model was, and given my biology and my chemistry, and my life's experiences, and my learning disabilities (we all have some), given all those handicaps, **I'm doing the best I can**."

Believe in your own activities. Listen for feedback and change when it is appropriate. But if you are on a track that seems overwhelming to another, this track may not be so horrendous for you. Feeding our own emotional bank account is a very individualized thing. Some of us crave order, some excitement, some peace, some challenge, some innovation, some fairness, some change and some of you want 'sameness.' My goals will not fit in your wish list; yours may topple or underwhelm mine.

So hold on to your dreams. As the Stanford Business Professor James Collins, who wrote the book, *Vital and Enduring Companies,* says, "Make your visions bold and audacious!"

Bold and audacious! I love that. Err on the side of idealism or grandiosity if you are, by nature, humble. Don't stop too soon, too short or too close to the top. Pace yourself. If you need lots of rest, reassurance, recreation, and the person next to you does not, stay on your own journey.

We all pace in different methods. I need lots of interruptions and short deadlines. Others need steady courses with lots of room for far-reaching conclusions. I'd rather write an article due tomorrow noon than for a month from now. Some of you would faint if asked to have anything done by tomorrow noon. We are all different. We are all okay.

Now, the dilemma rears its two heads when your pacing and your boss's, mate's or colleague's are drastically different! If you are not like me, and enjoy a slower pace, try, "I work best without imminent pressure, Jean. Please get the best from me by trying to plan ahead. And I will try to help you with that, by going over schedules with you periodically so I am not surprised with a short deadline for me."

It's imperative that you coach your boss or anyone whom you work around. Help them to learn to work best around you so that they can get the best from you. This is not demanding change. This is simply giving the data. If your boss or others sabotage the relationship by ignoring your feedback, that is another dilemma. By the way, optimists are not masochists. They get out if they have tried every possible solution to inspire change.

In the meantime, ask for what you want. Good optimists are not afraid to ask again and again, until they are sure the other person heard but simply can't or won't cooperate. Don't forget to reinforce an approximation of success if your colleague comes even close to cooperating with you. "John, I appreciate your effort. You really tried to do this in my style, and I know that was a sacrifice for you. I'll try to make it worth your efforts. Thanks."

Dr. Tom Byers, President, Slate Corporation, practices optimism. He is so excited about his company and his product that you want to go buy it. He also understands differences in working styles, and even takes a look at his own liabilities with vigor.

Mike Kolsdorf, Executive Vice President, CFO, Gerber Alley, another of the youngest senior executives in the country, knows his own working style—and negotiates it with others on a regular basis. His positive approach to his activities at his Atlanta company in contagious.

Makes It Fun

It can be fun to be the leader if you don't insist on being the perfect leader. Successful leaders all have their liabilities; they are all a little skewed, weak in some areas, biased, too focused, too unfocused, too liberal or too conservative. So are you.

When you get feedback that you are not perfect, salute the information. Try to do what you can if it seems appropriate, or especially if you have heard it before. If the feedback is off the mark, or hurts in some tiny recessed portion of old history, don't spend time on it. Your dissenter may be projecting on you. It simply may be junk.

Optimists never say, "That's just the way I am and I can't change."

An optimist will say, "I'm growing, changing, budding. I can change. I want to be in motion. I am not dead. Sometimes I am a little sleepy or stubborn, or just plain lazy. I am in the process, though. Thank you for the feedback."

Chapter 4

Human Resource Power Or Die!

Be A Member Of The Executive Business Team

My company, Growth & Leadership Center, has been meeting with Human Resource Directors for the past twelve years. I've come to believe that the human resource staff members are all too often relegated to the nice outer office of sweetness and light. They are only called in to the president or executive staff when someone in the company is going crazy and is a big threat to the legal and social welfare of the company.

If you are not on the executive business team, get there. Don't let business decisions be made about your company unless you are in the room. And conversely, don't make major policy decisions about your human resources unless you've tested the technical and financial outcomes with the operational staff of your organization.

You'd love to be part of the team, you claim. Then don't say: "They won't let me in."

If you are not in yet, I'll help you in with this book. The rest is up to you. Be patient. We are changing a culture—a technology-driven, control-oriented, authoritarian, male-dominated manager culture. In this chapter, thanks to the human resource people I know who have made it into that inner sanctum—and have made a difference—we will start your journey to the big mahogany, or metal or plastic doors of the executive suite.

We all enter the human resource field because we want to see people's lives enhanced. We want to bring the human touch to the business world. Or we want to train or recruit, or we just got in this field by accident. Time, bad management, bad supervisors, bad CEOs, technological convolutions, often dim those original good intentions.

Types of Human Resource Personnel

- ▲ Wimps—afraid of their shadow—nursery school aids
- ▲ 'Sweet' Ones—afraid of conflict, to speak out, stand out
- ▲ 'Dear' Ones—afraid to set limits, to say no.
- ▲ Whiners—know its wrong—just snivel
- ▲ Rebels—love to screw it up; want to make others wrong
- ▲ Dangerous—make fusses, lose, and HR loses too
- ▲ Stronger Ones—take stands, but give power back
- ▲ Courageous Ones—won't back down, but don't know how to compromise
- ▲ Smart Ones—find appropriate means to make a point—can't stand up—won't give away power!
- ▲ Powerful Ones—know the business; coach from the human view

Let's talk about the powerful ones: Yvette del Prado, Vice President, Tandem. She knows who can make decisions. She believes in the Big Picture, and is not afraid of change. Carleen Ellis, Vice President, Intel, calls a spade a spade. She sounds strong, walks strong, isn't afraid of men, machines and politics. Debbie Biondolillo, former Apple Vice President, now with GO, speaks out for individual power, made her own declarations of independence and does her homework. Jan Dahlin, HR Director, Micro Devices, continues to push for change. Lyndon Boone, Director of Staffing and Career Development at Cadence, is courageous and vigorous in her pursuits.

Herschel Kranitz, Vice President, Raynet, keeps and teaches a sense of humor in the business team and has the ear of the president. Sherry McVicar, Vice President, Read-Rite, with law background and business interests, picks colleagues who will look at the big business picture. Stephen Hams, HR Director, Hewlett Packard, is willing to address his own stumbling blocks and share them so the power team can learn and do something. Jennifer Koenecy, Vice President, HR, Silicon Graphics, considers the business aspects and knows the players, the products and the problems. Nita White-Ivy, HR Manager, Silicon Graphics, is innovative and courageous. Jack Fitzhenry, Vice President, HR, Apple International, is sensitive and sensible. The list goes on. It is an enormous list.

But there is a longer list. The list of those who have lost their spirit, fear the outcome of speaking the truth, or who have gotten tired of the battle of equality on the executive team.

How do you get on the executive team? First, you have to believe you belong there. Then believe that your constituents need you there. Lastly, believe that you have something to offer that group.

Jimmy Treybig, President, CEO, Tandem, brought together many of his top women candidates for Vice President of Tandem. In his own charming and dynamic way, he told each of them how strong they were and what potential they had for the company. And then he did them a big favor. He said that unless they really learned the technology of the products of the company, they could not rise to the top positions in the company. He did not say they needed to get EE degrees; he said they needed to learn what Tandem makes, read data sheets, take some of the basic courses and **be conversant** on every aspect of what Tandem does.

Treybig had the courage to tell the truth. Some of the women got discouraged and said they did not want to work that hard. Others are using the information, becoming more broad in their approach, and the smart ones are eternally grateful for the straight talk.

Prerequisites To Being Part Of The Team:

Know Your Company

Read the annual report. Learn the names. Go to board meetings or stock holder's meetings whenever you can. I get sick when someone tells me she or he is too tired to do the political meetings of her company, but will spend until 8 pm on a Friday night doing a micro-quarterly report which only the direct manager may see.

Work Smart And Not Long

Use your time well. Prioritize so that your time is spent on the big picture as well as the tasks at hand. Make sure that you are pleasing those who count; not your obstinate customer, your lazy colleagues, your administrative assistant or your own compulsive needs.

Compulsivity is a career killer. If you have to cross off every item on your list, and you have not prioritized, from A, B, C, tasks, you are being wasteful of your time. Be efficient. Look at your goals, and work within them. If going to that particular training doesn't fit in with the incremental goals toward a seat on the executive team, don't go!

Learn The Business Picture

Sit in on production meetings. Take every opportunity that is not Human Resources oriented. Learn the technology, the financial issues, the cash flow and budgeting dilemmas. Learn the financial challenges of your organization. Even non-profit organizations have financial worries and complexities. Interview the controller; you'd be surprised how he would like to take a break and talk to the wide-eyed you. Debbie Coleman, Apple Vice President, was the CFO and had a stint at manufacturing for years. She knows the product, the financial picture, and she made it a point to listen to and become friends with the sales and human resource people as well.

Find out what you don't know.

Be Political

I spend half of my counseling hours teaching people how to be political. All this means is learning:

- ▲ to read people
- ▲ to discover who is really in charge
- ▲ to assess the power base
- ▲ to understand what others want
- ▲ to understand why others want it

Sometimes the secretary to the General Manager has more power than he has. Often the manufacturing supervisor has more power than the Vice President, Engineering.

Learn people, and give them the following:

- ▲ reports
- ▲ feedback
- ▲ bad news

—in their form—not your own! Find the other person's form, style, manner, working style, passions, prejudices, and try to report in a way which he or she can hear the information.

Know Your Political Target: Is He Or She:

- ▲ a morning or night person—know when to deliver bad news
- ▲ a pragmatist or idealist—start with "I know we have only. . ." or "If only. . ."

▲ a listener or a talker—"I'd like to tell you—" or, "What do you think?"

▲ an auditory or visual—deliver the report orally, or, in print

▲ a reactionary or conservative—"Damn, Dave, this is. . ." Or, "Now, Dave, I know in the long run. . ."

▲ controlling or democratic—"Here are your figures. . ." or "I thought I'd show you the following."

Campaign For More Responsibility And Influence

Volunteer for new tasks. It's often easier to be chair person than to be a committee member. Assume responsibility. Ask to be on task forces. Start one. Ask to go with boss. Meet with those who make decisions. Sound like a decision-maker.

Be Patient

Your ascendancy to the business executive team may take some time. It may take a change in companies. But make it a goal. Give yourself time to make mistakes, political blunders and stupid decisions. Use all of the experiences to equip you for the executive team.

Gail Parker, Director, HR, EPRI, has the president's ear. He tells her that every business decision is a people issue. She also networks on a national level—keeps leading edge ideas on the table. What a team!

Get What You Need

Seventy-five percent of the human resource people I meet need sales training. They can't sell themselves, no less their ideas, their projects, their people. Many need assertiveness training, and many more need underpinnings of business management. You don't need an MBA, but if you think you do, go get it. If you want the MBA, but you haven't even got an undergraduate degree, go get one. That first three unit course is the beginning. Five years from now you may still be complaining, unless you start opening your own doors now.

Talk To The President!

Find the way to talk to the power broker in your company. Sometimes it is not the president. Then find a way to talk to this power person in your company. It may be the CEO or the Marketing or Financial VP, but find the person who can make decisions. When you find him or her, I've got some ideas for you:

Talk this person's language. Let him know that you have the interest of the organization at heart. Give him some ideas. Do your homework and then present your ideas. Don't be too audacious at this point, but try to get his attention, with, "I think our company picnics could be used as starting points for getting to know you better. Having a water can fall on your head doesn't really expose you to us. It's just funny; not engaging."

Or, suggest that morale could be spiked in engineering with some visual progress charts. Or that the company's hiring policy for women needs to be heralded and here's how:

When you've got his attention, show your optimism, about the president, the position, the company, or at the least, your opportunity with the company. When he walks away, he needs to remember what a inspiration you were.

Don't lie. Remember your own principles, but if you can say something positive about the president, the person, you will have created some memory points. Here are some examples when it is difficult to be directly complimentary:

▲ "You've got a horrendous job. I admire you for hanging in there."

▲ "It's an inspiration to know that you do not show your discouragement when I know the company has had its ups and downs."

▲ "I admire your consistency. We know what to expect from you and that makes it easier to work here."

▲ "Your passion for our product is a boost to my morale every day. I like knowing you believe in this work."

You have not been overtly complimentary. You may not even believe he is a good administrator, but you can't change him unless you get his attention. We don't get good attention with "I've been wanting to tell you what a first class jerk you are." Not only does that get negative attention, but it is impossible to recoup with anything that follows.

When you've done your introductory positive statements, and you have this person's attention, then, only then, begin to make your personal sales pitch on whatever you need. Remember, though, to accompany complaints with suggestions, and always to re-frame a negative situation with a positive outcome. "The company is at the wall right now, but 'the fittest will survive,' and this gives us a chance to test many nebulous assumptions we've been living with for a long time. I even have a little test I've designed to assess morale versus change-ratio capacity."

Now, maybe the test is awful—too immature and unsophisticated and not test-wise. But what you have done is present a concept. Maybe the president will want to design his own test, or have one done professionally, but you have planted some seeds and he is going to remember you for it.

Lastly, keep campaigning for people power. If you don't do your job and affect a change in thinking by the powers that be, your position will die. Your job description just fades away. Find a way to make an impact. Do surveys, studies, charts, interviews. Know that you are in the right position to remind everyone in every meeting, at every coffee hour or office party, that organizations have not been using people at their highest capacity.

You are the spokesperson for every employee and his mental and physical health. Why? Because appropriate use of human resources is your charter. Don't forget it. Be the conscience for your company. Always sell people power. That's your job—not just the benefits plan, the holiday party, training—your job is people power!

High Tech Equals Low Tech

Plan on teaching folks that the people product is as important as the tangible high tech product. Find ways to remind your organization that a thousand faces made the product going out the door. Use pictures of people. Do graphs with brain power or man power or woman power. Do charts with families and numbers of children that espouse or use or benefit by, or are a benefit to, this organization.

In every meeting, raise the consciousness of your technical colleagues that people need encouragement, challenge, information, inspiration and interactive skills. When you see an interchange in a meeting that doesn't go well, bring it to the attention of the players that participated in the interaction.

Be cautious about putting people on the spot. Don't make scenes and don't embarrass even the insensitive offender. They don't learn that way. They hurt with humiliation, and the humiliation eventually evolves into anger and persecution. Find a way to make your appraisal in a private spot, or with permission.

If you get permission to confront in the presence of others, the player's ego must be strong enough to watch the questionable interaction go under your microscope. When you can put the interaction under this scrutiny, let everyone see that it is the system of interplay, not just one obscene gesture or remark, that tipped the scales. Here's an example:

"Joe, when you asked Mark if we were going to expect the same delays as the last shipment, you were setting up a negative expectation."

At this juncture, I'll call *Opportunity #1,* you could have said, "Mark, I know that you are going to be able to handle this shipment because I'll bet you all benefited from the experience of the last time."

What usually happens is that Mark heard the first judgmental question and responded with, "Joe, we do the best we can, in spite of the screwed up inventory program you instituted."

Mark had *Opportunity #2:* He could have responded with:

"Joe, I know you were disappointed last time with the delay, but we've rehearsed and rehearsed and we know what went wrong and we won't let it happen this time. Your inventory program can be a big help in the long run. We still are not using it to our best interests and I'd like to talk to you about that when you have time."

These opportunities are like volleys in a volleyball game. The more volleys you can have on a particular subject, the more interactive and thrilling the game. Those slam dunks or balls hit out of the court really prevent a positive interaction.

Opportunity or Volley #3:
Mark: "You are full of it." Or:

Opportunity #3: "You could be right."

Opportunity or Volley #4
Joe: "Stop passing the buck." Or:

Opportunity #4: "Let's put our heads together."

Opportunity or Volley #5:

Mark: "You're impossible to work with." Or:

    Opportunity #5: "We've got some work to do together so we both feel hopeful and trusting."

Opportunity Volley #6

Joe: "I'm leaving this unproductive meeting." Or:

    Opportunity #6. "It's rough right now for us, but I think we can put these ideas together."

Point out when encouragement is not being fostered. Coach that when the human potential is not being considered, your organization's bottom line is at stake. Be the teacher. Teach reinforcement for an approximation of success. Coach managers to really listen to employees. Teach reflective listening.

    Reflective Listening is about giving feedback about the other person's perception. It is not about answering. Not yet. It is not about defending yourself. Not yet. It is allowing him to know you understand his point of view. We all talk about how much people want to be loved or needed. I believe that, most of all, we want to be understood. I think I'll make that even stronger. We want to be understood just as much as we want to be loved. Love is generic, amorphic, ambiguous. Understanding is often much more important.

    So: **Reflective Listening**:

- ▲   you don't have to agree, apologize or promise anything
- ▲   don't deny the other's perception or reality
- ▲   don't distract away from his view
- ▲   don't defend yourself or the situation
- ▲   don't problem solve

Enabling Is A Form Of Being Pessimistic

Organizations need to teach understanding. Companies and human resources personnel, on the other hand, can be enabling or addictive organizations which take more than their share of the employee's point of view.

Educate your colleagues when your company is 'babying' its employees. My management consulting experience has surprised me with the conclusion that companies tend to coddle or enable problem employees more than they set limits for difficult employees.

I hate to use the overworked 'co-dependent' word. If you've been working in the out-back and you haven't heard it yet, it simply means someone who is addicted to helping someone else. If you or your colleagues, in the name of helping, think of others instead of themselves some of the time, call them on it. Teach about the theory of—'symbiosis,' and the disease of enabling others.

Sometimes an employee is emotionally blackmailing a manager or a peer. Your job is to see through this and help the victim of this manipulation to see what he can do to stop the blackmail. Calling people on both sides of this triangle takes courage. Hold your ground. It hurts a lot to have a self-serving style analyzed for what it really is. You may be the bearer of bad tidings.

I still remember the person who first reminded me of my own enabling ways. I am grateful to her. And it hurt.

If you have some of the enabling qualities, please ask colleagues to check you on some of your perceptions or decisions. It's easy, especially in this field, to become employee care-takers.

Setting the limit, defining that fine line often takes an objective viewpoint, usually from someone not so close to your employee.

Technical People Aren't Trained To People Watch—You Are!

Your job is to teach optimism if the company is missing this component. First you may decide you have to believe in it your self. This may take a little doing if you are trained in helplessness. When you decide that you are more productive being an optimist, you can then sell this to all your colleagues. Remember that:

- ▲ Optimists live longer (cancer group studies)
- ▲ Optimists sell more (Blue Cross insurance studies)
- ▲ Optimists sell more over the long haul (Blue Cross studies)
- ▲ Optimists sleep better (Type A personality research)
- ▲ Optimists look better (smile muscles versus frown muscles
- ▲ Optimists are promoted (they inspire enthusiasm)

So, if you've convinced yourself to think optimistically, your job is to sell this behavior to everyone with whom you come in contact.

Why is it so hard to maintain optimism? Because there are so many opportunities to be measured, to fail, to flail, to be wrong, to be blamed, to be assessed, and so few opportunities to be right, perfect, okay, enough.

Measurement Tests:
- ▲ periodic reviews and promotion criteria
- ▲ traffic lights and turns and highway speed
- ▲ income tax and CPAs who help you with yours
- ▲ schoolrooms and teachers
- ▲ colleges and professors
- ▲ lovers and mates
- ▲ parents and kids
- ▲ weight clinics or spas
- ▲ measuring tapes and mirrors
- ▲ class reunions and old friends
- ▲ your penmanship, your work tasks, your answers in Jeopardy, Trivial Pursuit, Bridge, Pinnacle, Gin Rummy, Chinese Checkers

Compensating positive opportunities can begin to make up for the everyday measurement tools we are shrouded by. Teach your team to accentuate the positive, to talk like an optimist and to begin to believe that things can be re-framed or re-worked or re-formed or re-defined!

Remind managers to write thank you notes, supervisors to give the 'atta boy, atta girl' comments, to point out the good works of others. I recently saw Bruce Jenner, Decathlon winner, commenting on Carl Lewis. Bruce claimed, "Carl is probably the best athlete of all time." This did not detract from Bruce's title of the best all around Olympian of his day. He pointed the wand in Carl's direction. Carl won't forget it. The audience won't either. And

Bruce will be remembered as the one who was qualified to say it.

This all seems so simple or obsequious to you? Well, just try it for awhile. We are acclimatized to remember the negative about us. With all those measurement tools around us, it takes several positives to make up for our daily supply of negative tests. Do we get enough positives? Of course not.

Teach others what you need. People worry about being pathetic or sounding too vulnerable. My experience is that the 'tough fragile' who is afraid of this is usually showing only the tough side. Err on the side of the vulnerable. You will probably feel more uncomfortable than the one who is experiencing your revelations.

Set the seeds for what you want. They may not grow easily. But set the seeds, water and fertilize, and keep reinforcing, with: "Gosh, Liz your announcement really congratulated the FAB Department. I'm impressed with the way you gave them so much credit. Good work!"

When you get discouraged with your job, remind yourself about how important your task is. Remind yourself about the industrial revolution, the information revolution, and now the slower and more subtle, human revolution, where people may come before industry and information.

When you get down in the dumps because the bottom line translates to product and not people, or that science and technology seem to have more to do with hardware than 'peopleware,' ready your own mentor or cheerleading team. Have people you can call and say, "Hey, these hard-liners are laughing at me again. They don't get it. Will you tell me I'm on the right track even if they don't know it?"

International

And then when your agent, cheerleader, friends soothes you, listen up!

About The Model HR Model

Recently I've been interviewing successful HR individuals, for two talks I'm giving in the next few months, and for this book. I came across my finest interview last week, and I want to tell you about her.

Sherry McVicar is Vice President, Human Resources, at Read-Rite Corporation, a company that struggled, with down-turns, turn -around teams, and now is profitable, international and public. Sherry didn't make all that happen. But, the company went from 800 people to 6,600 in the last year or so, and Sherry has been there that long. The gross sales have multiplied in staggering degrees and the company looks like it is on the way. Sherry is one of the stars. *Inc. Magazine* named Read-Rite the fastest growing company in the world.

She was recruited by the CEO, Cyril Yansouni, who had worked with Sherry at several companies before this. Cyril had a mentor, Paul Ely, Convergent Technologies guru, and Sherry's mentor has been Cyril and other business executives. She watches how business really works.

Paul had twenty years of Hewlett Packard indoctrination and then the frenzy of a smaller company. He learned. He taught. Cyril learned. He taught. And it seems that Sherry is learning and teaching.

Sherry looks and acts like a business person. She is direct, enthusiastic, energetic and open. She seems confident. She admits mistakes and is also fun to be with. She explained that she had learned from companies that struggled, Qume, and companies that merged, Convergent and Unisys, and she knows when something feels good. She had to experience the pain to know the joy of positive birth.

Too many of us are afraid of the pain. We don't want personal labor pains and we don't want to be in the presence of company labor pains. So we 'jump ship' if things are getting tough, instead of deciding to learn as much as we can from the drama at hand. Even established organizations go through transitions and trauma. IBM employees are currently excited about some of the changes and growth spurts IBM is taking.

Back to Sherry. Sherry believes in the business of the company. She is not afraid of reading financial sheets, claims it is necessary, and wants to be part of every business decision. Her CEO believes she ought to be too! What a perfect combination. The leader who wants the HR ear, and the HR who wants to know exactly what is going on with the company.

Sherry is an equal member of Line Management. Her people attend every major staff meeting in the company. She trains them to think legal, think financial, and, of course, to continue to think people.

She was able to recruit colleagues from past companies to work in this new arena. She trusts them and they trust her. They can work together with the 'Shorthand' from other projects and other companies. They do not have to continue to prove themselves to each other. And they know and admit their shortcomings. Oh, what a team.

Our teams and our organizations do not have to be perfect. We just have to be perfect at resourcing our complimentary team players. At our company, GLC, I am a **'quick start,'** from Kathy Kolbe's book, *Conative Connection.* I have surrounded myself with Aj Kessler, my **'data gatherer,'** Dick Spath, my **'follow through,'** and Joan Blake and a host of other team members who can **'implement'** my **'quick start'** ideas.

Kathy Kolbe believes that we have a basic working style preference. We inherently work best as a **"quick start, data gatherer, follow through** or **implementor."** We can work out of all the four preference styles, but if our basic and preferred working style is used the most, we become satisfied, nurtured and productive.

If we have to work in our least preferred working style, having to use tools which do not come as naturally to us, we become stifled, strained and un-productive. If I had to do research or accounting all day, or had to follow up on all the projects I start, I would be miserable.

Back to Sherry. Her staff members are selected to complement each other. She insists that HR is part of the business team. She trains her people to serve their constituents, not sit in off-site retreats thinking up ideas that managers may not have a need for, or may not see how they fit in the big picture.

She teaches her staff to get buy-in every step of the way. Don't run off with this wonderful idea you have unless you have convinced a decision-maker that it is necessary. All too often other human resource personnel will believe your ideas are timely and essential. But sell the idea to the group who has to use it and may not want to.

This is why you need sales and persuasive skills to be good in HR. Learn how to express your ideas and persuade others to consider the plan. Then learn how to negotiate differences and close the deal. If you haven't got these skills or don't want to obtain them, hang up your hat and volunteer for work in a nunnery where you may not have to experience change.

So what does it take to have a good HR team:

- ▲ people who read their constituents
- ▲ people who get 'buy-in' from constituents
- ▲ people who strive for equality in all business decisions.
- ▲ people who sit in cross sections of the business
- ▲ people who trust each other
- ▲ people who know the individual strength of teammates
- ▲ people who are brave, state opinions and sell them

Good luck if you are already on the optimistic team. Good luck on your win. If you aren't on that team yet, don't despair. In either case, you've got goals to work toward. The act of working toward that goal is the prime energy producer. Reaching, scratching, campaigning, moving in any direction at all—the act itself can be stimulating, hope-producing and even satisfying.

Helplessness is poison. Power is the ability to feel you can act. If you still don't feel optimistic after reading this chapter, or if it all feels like too much work, please change fields.

Human Resource people have the power to change the way people work, the way people think about work, and the way people work about thinking. Give it your best.

Our mission statement for Growth & Leadership Center is:

GLC will stimulate the Good Life for everyone who walks through the door—and will provide the Good Life for its staff members.

The last line is important. We want to support crisis, exchange tasks, do baby-sitting, pick up out of town guests, tutor for the boards, listen to marital problems, increase resources, and offer the best that we can offer to our staff. Are we good at it? Not really. Not yet—but we want to be. We are getting better. Survival mode falls on us sometimes, too, and we forget the good life for our staff. But we can't give up on that. Neither can you, for your staff, your employees, your organization, and especially for you.

If this chapter stimulated you, take your boss to lunch. Talk about being different. Tell him you just woke up from a long nap.

If this chapter only reminds you of what a good job you are doing, get the boss to take you to lunch. He's got a star!

Chapter 5

What To Do With Pessimists

Teach That 'No' Is A Dirty Word

Pessimists live in fear that they will do something wrong. So they do nothing! When you are preparing a pessimist to say 'yes,' warn him that it will be all right if the project does not turn out perfectly. Give him lots of qualifiers to prepare him: "Not everyone can do this." Or, "This is a job which may have to have several rough drafts or re-works." Or, "I'm not sure I could do this the first time myself."

When I talk about Pessimists in this chapter, I am talking about the helpless pessimist who feels powerless. There are qualities of pessimism, I must remind you, **that are realistic and importantly conservative** and important in any organization. We want the person on board who will give this reality check.

In this chapter, however, I am describing the unhealthy pessimist who does not become a check point for conservatism, but pulls the whole team down with his despair and inactivity.

There are people in between. And, most importantly, people change. Falling in love can change the grumpiest guy in the office. The right title or position can change Ms. Negative into 'Le Cooperative!'

To begin to transform a pessimist, arm him with enough qualifiers to help him to feel hopeful about something. With qualifiers, your helpless person can decide it is all right to try the event or task. These doubters are usually so ridden with failure phobia and internal judges that it is hard to ask them to attempt any new behavior. Reduce the risk by upping the odds that he can win with any of the discounters you can offer him.

The pessimist is afraid to do anything humiliating. Coach him with: "Gosh, this a squishy kind of an assignment, Fred. Don't worry if you fall on your face this time."

Once more you are teaching that one strike does not end the game. In baseball, you will watch coaches who highly encourage the batter after the first and second strike. They are pushing confidence that the next pitch will be a hit, and not the third strike.

Give your pessimists strike one and two. Allow that mistakes happen—that they are actually in the process of making a successful attempt.

Teach the person who has learned helplessness from parents, former bosses or extenuating circumstances of his own, that he can become a **can do** person. Even if you are doubtful yourself, push yourself to be the coach for this ill-motivated victim. Give him extra confidence. His emotional bank account is very low, so he will need some extra credits to get the proceeds of his work moving. Take the time to coach this slow learner.

Do people really change? Of course they do. Miracles happen every day in my office. In my classes, I even have evidence of these miracles.

I did an **Anger Expression Training** for seven executives recently. Each thought he could never express anger appropriately. Half of them were desperately afraid of conflict; the other half had no positive experience with their outrageous temper tantrums.

Within seven hours, these people changed permanently. I couldn't be in the field of change if I did not have daily examples of forms of change:

- ▲ Company presidents learn to delegate.
- ▲ Secretaries learn to ask for what they want.
- ▲ Wives learn, before divorce, to ask for their share.
- ▲ Unemotional men learn to express feelings.
- ▲ Narcissists learn to give and share and care.
- ▲ Shy people get assertive.
- ▲ Workaholics learn to balance.
- ▲ 'Drivers' learn to relax.
- ▲ Passive folks learn to initiate.

A positive experience can erase a lifetime of negative ones. Help create a win for your hesitant pessimist. Teach him to say 'yes' and then to plan to assist him with the homework to do after the yes.

Teach That 'Yes' Can Also Be a Dirty Word

Unempowered people say 'yes' because they want to please. They are afraid of the negative consequences that a 'no' can mean to them. To avoid conflict they will stall and do anything rather than confront the requester. To avoid conflict, they will move to Alabama, take demotions, eat unwarranted criticism, and hide their resentment with passive aggressive behavior. So, teach that being a positive and assertive person can allow you to set limits, and to resist having to please or avoid conflict.

Teach that 'no' can be a powerful word which shows responsibility for your time, energy, other resources. Enabling managers or bosses or employees who do more of their share, who do another's work, who can't say no, are damaging to an organization. Eventually they feel resentful, and if they are the helpless type, they will go 'back door' with their anger. How? They will be late, forget, avoid the meetings, do behind the scenes maneuvers, and will create morale problems by sniping and whimpering around the edges.

Too many yes's which may not coincide with a priority list, can kill an organization, a group or a person. Watch the 'yes' and use it only when it meets your values, your priority goals, and if you have the time and energy for the experience. Some of us say 'yes' just because the 'yes' will feel good or be an ego boost. Those 'warm fuzzies' are good motivators sometimes, and need to be on your priority list as well, but keep the balance.

Sometimes I just want to horse around or play with a group of people I love, and it may not be in the best interest of my business, but it can be in the best interest of my emotional health. Be discreet with the 'yes.'

Sell The Doctrine

Persuade your pessimists to adopt your mission. The mission, of course, needs to be in their best interests too. Guy Kawasaki, *Selling The Dream,* teaches that you must evangelize your own dream and then teach others to evangelize also. James Collins, *Eighteen Vital and Enduring Companies,* Stanford Business Professor, teaches companies to be make their mission world-shaking and visionary. The doctrine needs a philosophical and idealistic goal which can inspire others. "We will upgrade the first four months of all infants in the world" may be a pretty lofty mission, but who would want to ignore this objective?

The doctrine needs to be splashed all over your environment and it needs to be positive. **Reducing Poverty** does not sound as hopeful as **Creating Resources.** Behavioral psychology theory of learning reminds us that our subconscious doesn't always hear the 'don't.' Our psyche just hears, "Get run over in the street." So saying, "Stay on the sidewalk," is a healthier command.

Persuade your people to love the doctrine or change it. Ask for help. I always tell my new staff members at our center that we have not figured out the ultimate formula for our kind of business. We are always open to change. "Don't be afraid to suggest," I remind new people. "We are not perfect—we are not even close. In fact, some of what I do does not work well at all." And that is the truth!

Screen Out Those Who Can't

If you have given your pessimist all you can give, and you see no sign of optimism, ask him to leave. Do not pour energy into someone who may not be capable of your doctrine at this moment in time. Optimists cut their losses. They are not masochistic enough to continue giving or coaching without some dividends.

If I'd had some of the bad breaks that I've heard from people who have lost loved ones, homes, companies and health, I might feel dreary too. Watch for the balance between what you can put into someone and the potential for getting something back.

I used to be the kind of person who actually tried to make lunch dates after I terminated someone from my company. I was so anxious about my own abandonment needs that I could not cleanly cut the cord. Good-byes are hard on many of us.

Some people are so phobic of endings that they cannot even go to the airport with loved ones. The turning point of my own professional career was when I learned to ask someone to leave and not try to seduce him into making it a wonderful occasion. I learned to accept another's feelings of anger and rejection. I no longer try to 'sweet-talk' them out of the genuine pain they feel. 'No' rarely feels great.

I was also addicted to making people happy, so I suffered when someone was mad or disappointed about the termination. I've finally learned that you cannot say 'no' to someone and expect that they will like it. Oh, yes, later they may say that the termination was the best thing that ever happened to them, but at the immediate point of 'no' impact, we all shudder and feel hurt or mad. Lashing out at the 'no' perpetrator feels good. I know that now, expect it, and I have stopped taking it personally.

Move away from people who won't grow. If they say, "I've always been like this" or "I've done it this way for forty years," give them your best change sermons, and if they don't get it, go away.

Rub up against winners. Buy lunch for the person who can cope with the incorrigible boss. Find out why Harold can take all those moves, or why Roger copes with the working conditions and seems happy. Think of yourself as being in a concentration camp. Some of you suffer as much in your work life as if you were in a camp. Then look around for the person who seems to be handling the camp life the best.

What are these optimists doing to cope, to keep their spirits up, to boost the morale of others, to keep the pace when things are bad? Spend time with those winners, not the losers who carp and whine and can't think of a single solution for themselves.

Save The Salvageables, Quickly

If you see someone with potential, who seems to display the qualities of the pessimist, give him a big dose, quickly, of the optimist in you. Pessimism can be so pervasive it spans many categories of one's life. Or it can be limited to one or two areas of a person's life. Teach him that he can be awful in one arena and pretty good in some others.

If he only applies pessimism over issues which he can take personally, you will want to help him to see that he may be over-identifying with poor results. Test him to see if he accepts as much responsibility over the positive outcomes. Usually we don't. We really feel culpable for failures. If things work out, we believe it may be a fluke, or we distribute the glory to a team of others.

The same pessimist may only be pessimistic by applying failure in one area with the belief that he will always be a failure in that **one arena**. He may feel if he has a disappointment in one category, he will always have failure in love, or in negotiations, or in small talk, or in athletic events. Help him to see that this form of permanent thinking about one area is really not healthy. I saw the 100 pound weakling become a roller hockey star. I've seen unlucky-in-love folks turn into great mate material. Poor negotiators can learn that science in no time.

Dr. Martin Seligman believes that optimism and pessimism slide down three separate scales: Pervasiveness, Permanency, and Personalization. If you believe you or someone you care about is falling into the hopelessness hole, catch him quickly. Teach about the three forms of optimism, and see if you both can analyze ways that you categorize your helplessness and ways that you personalize your optimism or pessimism.

Do not spend too much time or energy if he cannot get your point. "Look, Peter, you have potential. I will coach you one hour a week for four weeks. If you have not made the incremental changes we agree upon, I have to give up on you."

Each of us needs reinforcement. Usually we need it immediately. That's why a fourth of a pound of weight loss does not always inspire enough to keep the ice cream out of the plate. The reward has to be visible or touchable or feel good. Don't spend too much time on someone who will not pay you back with small approximations of success.

Remember that coaches need good strokes too. Ask for whatever you need to be able to keep the mentoring up. Don't be the victim of a starving mentee who never gets enough. You deserve thanks and reinforcement and you can get it.

Coach What To Do When Evaluations Hurt

"John, you are brilliant on the project, but—you don't take criticism. You sometimes miss the big picture."

"Bob, you are VP potential with this company, but you create tension around some of the collaborating team."

"Jane, you are technically strong, but you miss deadlines too frequently."

No matter what is said about your personal or technical competence, you probably don't like negative criticism when you hear it or read it. In fact, if you are the average human being, you won't like criticism  in any form! Three common feelings usually trigger the dreaded reflex to poor reviews:

I. You Feel Misunderstood

This hurts. You feel your manager misread your intentions, or more probably, you experience double messages. "Get the job done," you heard. You also heard, "and make everybody happy while you are doing it!"

2. You Feel Rejected

How could your boss do this? You feel dumped. You believed you were on track, you hadn't heard many complaints, and you thought you were one of the favorite sons or daughters. The review shows you are no longer fair-haired!

3. You Feel Scared

If you can be surprised about this, perhaps there are other surprises in store for you. "What else have I missed?" you worry. Fear is a powerful emotion which creates paranoid-sounding responses and an inability to risk. Poor ratings can make you afraid in some over-generalized forms.

Why are we so attached to our tasks? The reasons we take our evaluations so personally is that we have become a culture of conscientious achievers. We attach these tasks to our psyches so closely that our egos cannot disengage from them without major surgery! We can't help it. We've been programmed. Schools, colleges, companies all encourage exceptional ego orientation to our tasks.

Here in Silicon Valley, and particularly for the engineers in this valley, we are a community of high profile magicians! Miracles are expected; continued creativity is the goal! We are designed to design the best!

But, sometimes there is slippage; occasionally our priorities do not meet those of the powers that be. Periodically we only 'selectively listen' to the directions, the bosses' values, the company's deadlines.

We Confuse Excellence With Perfection

Make your best effort. Don't kill yourself for perfection. Perfection is never attainable for the compulsive person who always has one more hurdle for your race. Hurdles need to be spaced in distances which allow for *stride recovery.* If you or someone else is expecting too much of you, you may not be able to take criticism. A lowered evaluation, even though you are having life strains, company reorganizations or difficult colleagues, can be esteem-wrecking. It does not have to be career-wrecking.

Give **you** a break. If you feel you've done all you can, rest up. If you feel the evaluation is on target, don't punish you any more than the evaluation does. **And,** get started on a plan to improve on every line item on the review!

What Can One Do About A Poor Evaluation?

1. Appeal

Don't give up easily. Ask for a second or third meeting. Assure your evaluator that you have learned some strong lessons from the review. You want to negotiate the misunderstanding or the crossed signals. It is your job to sell your boss on the work that you have done. Don't claim that the boss also has a responsibility for the final outcome of the communication! This is, of course, true, but we are not always privileged with wise supervisors. Help yours along!

But do hint that in the future you are willing to bend over backwards to assure that both of you understand the priorities.

Remind your supervisor that, "I want you to take in to account my excellent work on the 'Signal 7' project." Bring in your statistics, letters of thanks or recommendation, a typical work day, the schedule you followed. 'Credentialize' yourself with your evaluator!

2. Re-Frame the Consequences

Make the best of the bad news! You may choose to learn from the situation, to use this as a turning point. Even if the evaluation leads to your quest for another company, look upon the review as good news, the perfect catalyst to look for the new work scope, or, as a reminder of work behavior, you may badly need to put into practice.

3. Complain

Make a fuss; don't eat it. If you really feel that the review is unjustified, get a friend or colleague to read the review over with you and then encourage honest feedback. Secondly, take the review to yet another resource who may give you more constructive suggestions. If those people still believe you have a justifiable complaint, do so—complain!

Gently ask for a capitulation of your review. Suggest at the onset that you recognize that there may be no final changes, but that you believe you deserve the time to voice your objections. Expect that the outcome may only be a hearing; that numbers may not change, but convince yourself that you are setting seeds with the boss to be used later—the next evaluation, the next round.

4. Use This As a Time to Make a Change!

If the evaluation follows a series of other disappointments, misunderstandings, missed raises or unhappy meetings, use this moment to make the job change you probably need.

5. Ignore the Whole Thing—Get On the Next Project—And Forget It

Get busy. Your next evaluation may make up for this bleak moment in history. Don't give a lot of energy to this review. You have bigger work to do, more important projects to finish, more vital people to impress.

6. Give Yourself a Monthly Evaluation

Try to get boss to buy in to the idea. But make it easy for the boss; just show your own evaluation with 'agree' or 'disagree' boxes to fill in. This allows you to rank your priority issues and gives you both some new criteria for next time.

7. Ask For Formal Evaluations On a More Regular Basis

If you can increase immediate feedback levels, you will have a better barometer reading of you. But most managers **hate** to give reviews. Remind them that 'more often' may not mean 'more work.' Promise that you will take responsibility for getting forms ready, doing your share, and sticking it under the bosses' nose.

Even promise that you will make sure the meeting happens. "Why," you wail, "do I have to do so much of the work?" Because it is *your problem*, you don't like the review, you want a better one, you want to succeed! Stop griping; do it!

Lastly, look at the evaluation as a turning point for you. Behavioral changes happen when we are hit by a truck, face death, or face ego damage! Use this critical moment to find a new and exciting you. Take a communication class, find new ways to look at your job scope, learn to negotiate priorities with your manager, and seize the moment. Let this black letter day serve notice for the new era!

Pessimism is hard on an organization. Build optimists. After your best effort with a pessimist reaps too few rewards, ask him to leave. And don't try to take him to lunch.

Chapter 6

Rub Up Against Other Optimists

They Don't Worry About Comparisons

The Optimist Clubs of America, an international organization founded in 1919, have thousands of members, meet every day of the week in almost every town in the nation. This is a service club which fosters reinforcement for positive thinking. I met this happy organization when I was asked to speak at their luncheon meeting. Having presented at many similar lunch events, it was no big deal to me to walk into their meeting lobby. What was a big deal was the laughter, the fun, the smiling faces within. The laughter wasn't nervous or anxious. The laughter was coming from the stomach. They sounded happy.

This organization does everything right. They use rituals. Rituals, if not too drawn out, imprint the message. The **Optimist Creed** is, of course, positive. It is:

Promise Yourself—

▲   *To be so strong that nothing can disturb your peace of mind.*

▲   *To talk health, happiness and prosperity to every person you meet.*

▲   *To make all your friends feel that there is something in them.*

▲   *To look at the sunny side of everything and make your optimism come true.*

▲   *To think only of the best, to work only for the best and expect only the best.*

▲   *To be just as enthusiastic about the success of others as you are about your own.*

▲   *To forget the mistakes of the past and press on to the greater achievements of the future.*

▲   *To give so much time to the improvement of yourself that you have no time to criticize others.*

▲   *To be too large for worry, too noble for anger, too strong for fear, and too happy to permit the presence of trouble.*

Optimist members practice what they preach, bearing in mind a positive re-framing when they lose money selling Christmas trees.

One of the members may say: "Well, we helped a lot of happy and poor families when we gave the trees away the last night." Or he may say, "This was a good lesson for us. Is service making money to give away, or can service also be giving away our services instead of making money?"

When another member answers with, "Yeah, but we had to give away services and our own money too on this deal." The good Optimist member responds with, "What an opportunity for us—especially in the holiday season."

The Optimists believe in minor negative reinforcement. The Optimist Clubs highly reinforce when you do it right—with applause, stamping, shouts. On the negative reinforcement side, on the other hand, the Optimist members shape negative behavior more mildly. When a member announces a negative conclusion, he is fined. The amount of fine depends on how negative he was. They seem to learn rather quickly.

Whining Is Contagious

You could catch it. Transpose some letters, in whining, and you almost get *winning*. Winning is also contagious. Stay close to winners. Don't go to lunch with the scowling, complaining losers. Don't be afraid to ask someone who is doing it right for help. "You know, Tom, you seem to be the only one who is content with Barbara's management style. Can I take you to lunch so I can learn how you cope with it?"

If you see someone who apparently is unruffled by the layoff rumors, or seems to accept all the changes, or who gets along with the difficult employee, find out his secrets.

I'm not talking about the guy who copes so well that you aren't sure he is alive. He's the one who takes it all and hides his resentment. There is nothing good to learn from door-mats. Positive people are assertive and set limits. I'm talking about the person who genuinely seems to be able to master the difficult situation or colleague.

Let this optimist mentor you. Pick his brain. Learn his techniques, his philosophy. He seems to be doing it right. He is not sacrificing his principles and, yet, seems to be able to cooperate with a difficult situation. It is possible to learn to cope while keeping your dignity. Some optimists even believe that while it looks like coping, they are actually shaping new behavior in another's actions. Here is how this shaping is accomplished:

M&Ms Work!

Every time any difficult person comes even close to an approximation of the behavior you desire, reward it!

I know. We don't see many M&Ms being handed out in industry, but the rewards are much more subtle. Successful people reward others in almost every experience of their day. They say or do the following, when someone has approximated change:

- ▲ "Thanks, Harry, for calling back so promptly,"
- ▲ "This report is so much better than last quarters."
- ▲ "As difficult as it was, you've made a start."
- ▲ "I'm pleased you got this far, Charles."
- ▲ "Martha, I noticed you didn't let Larry get upset at this meeting."
- ▲ "Folks, you are getting closer to the target with each week."

Other Reinforcements:

- ▲ smiles
- ▲ nods
- ▲ moving forward, toward
- ▲ deferential body language. (I don't mean bowing. I mean moving your chair over politely when he moves by or next to you.)
- ▲ responding quickly
- ▲ eye contact
- ▲ placing his name first on a list

In order to quiet those of you who believe you are only reinforcing sub-level behavior, please be reassured that you are shaping the behavior toward the **ultimate desired goal.** Since positive reinforcement is more successful than negative reinforcement, and since optimists are **very patient**, shaping behavior works. They know there will be back-slides and 'Cha-Cha' dances (three steps forward, three back, and three in place), and they simply plan for those relapses.

You may have been raised or tutored in the good old school of: "If something is wrong, I'll tell you about it. If you don't hear anything, you know you are doing all right."

If you had that indoctrination, you are probably a reluctant candidate for reinforcing an approximation of success. Be assured, though, that behavioral science attests to the notion that positive reinforcement creates greater change in the long run. If you were one of these Henry Fonda types, consider changing. The man of few positive words is passé. Its fun to reward others. Kids learn faster. Adults learn faster. You may too!

What if there is no real change happening? If there is not continued improvement, you may decide the other person is sabotaging progress or is simply uncooperative. Optimists don't take the lack of progress in others personally. If you've done what you can, and when you can, and there is no substantial movement, you have to assume that the other person simply does not want to cooperate, learn, grow or change. This happens.

Optimists don't worry about comparing themselves to others, other projects, other organizations. They believe that each unit is unique, so there is no need to judge themselves or other standards which may disillusion or depress them. These positive organizations keep raising their own bar, allowing others to set standards which the optimists may use as guideposts.

Jealously or biased judgments don't happen as much for optimists. They believe in the philosophy of abundance. "There is always enough—sometimes it's just a little difficult to find it!"

Comparisons are simply data resources. They are not demands for change. You can look at what others are doing as a check point for yourself, but your own confidence may help you to see that the comparison is not always beneficial to your situation. If it is, use it. Don't use it as an internal judge though. We all have enough of those. Use it as a guide; something you strive for. The other organization's goal can also become yours. How many companies decided to be second to Hertz?

Coach your organization to believe that there is no other organization comparable to yours. Competition is the word for others who may do some of the things you do in some of the ways you do them. But you are not identical twins. You must believe that you have special attributes, your company or team has individualized talents that overlay some of the look-alike comparisons.

I'm writing this on Super Bowl Sunday, 1992. The Buffalo Bills believe they are unique because they have quarterback Jim Kelly, with the best record in franchise history. They have one heck of a stadium and fans which will follow them feverishly to Minneapolis.

The Bulls have Marv Levy, coach, while the Redskins have multi-dimensional Joe Gibbs, with his history of recent Super Bowl Games. The Washington Redskins also have a nearly balanced run and pass team, and rabid, enthusiastic fans who cross through cultural layers of congressmen and men of the streets.

Every organization, profit, non-profit, large or small, soft tech or high tech—each organization can declare and advertise its uniqueness.

Some organizations are wonderfully defensive; they plan, do proactive work and prepare for set-backs and offensive plays which may be placed on them. Other organizations have better offense. I'm thinking of Cypress Semiconductors, with the dynamic T.J. Rodgers as President. Rodgers pushes forward, does not keep his company in the wings, starts forward action and never stands in waiting. For every organization, defensive or offensive strength—each strength is an asset. Your organization may be conservative or liberal, customizing or large scale production, pragmatically managed or idealistically managed. You are unique. Name your assets. Plan around them. Capitalize on them. Publicize them.

When the business picture demanded short term counseling from centers like mine, I capitalized on our long term treatment mentality. We promoted our group as one who would not do assessment and referral work (EAPS–Employee Assistance Programs), because we believed in a treatment mentality which called for a little longer interaction between problems and interventions. We did not get the immediate assessment and referral business. We got what was left over. And that was enough.

Now we are even called on to do the EAP work for EAP groups. That means we counsel employees of those who do the counseling for companies. We became the doctor's doctor, and we love it. But do we do short term assessment and referral for these doctors? Did we subjugate our principles? You decide.

Yes, we conform to standard EAP requirements, always campaigning and espousing that we prefer the other style. Economically we know the problems, and we offer suggestions which could cut the costs. We do some innovative compromises right now for many companies. And we keep trying to shape the behaviors of companies that call on us. We are patient. We know that changing the way insurance companies and employers think will take time. We've got time. Optimistic Organizations always have time.

Shaping behavior in other people and organizations takes confidence and a lot of patience with small rewards. Just that these EAP companies call on us to do their counseling, in spite of our conflicting principles, is an approximation of success!

They Ask, "What Can My Organization Do For Me?"

Optimistic organizations look for people who will know how to use the company. The ideal employee or team member will know what he wants and will ask for it. He will see to it that there is a possibility of getting what he wants.

The organization needs that courageous individual who will contract with a give and take mentality. "I give the best of me and produce what you want, and you will try to give the best of the organization to me and try to produce for me."

Companies do give—with wages, benefits, sabbaticals, special privileges and recognition in the right places. What places are those? The places the employee or team member wants them placed in. Don't give a long vacation to the workaholic whose life is the company. Give him research hours or time to do outside projects which he thinks is beneficial to his company productivity. Don't give bonuses to the genius who has started four companies and has more money than he needs. Give him lab space or more recognition, or name a building after him.

It's vital to find out what the reward style can be. Don't give roses to those allergic to them. Don't give speeches to those who think that words are superficial. Don't 'glad-hand' the person who does not trust glad-handing.

As an organization, partner up with other companies doing it right. Exponentially multiply your end results to the power of two! Never be afraid to compare, to share, to open what you can open to another group.

I know. Don't give away company secrets. But be open to the process of sharing what is possible; sometimes it is mutual advertising, sometimes it is buying training which can be shared. Imagine companies for whom computers were not their products being able to share training costs with five other companies. The unit price would decrease. The optimistic employees would be impressed with the efficiency.

Each member of an organization owns the organization in some way. Some have stocks and partner shares. This is an easy way to be reminded that you are an owner. But the person without stock who worked the best years of his life for that organization is also a form of an owner. Take charge of your company. And hire or choose people who will have that sense of ownership even without the certificates which prove it. If you are not a financial owner yet, act as if you were. Showing that sense of ownership to others is very exciting to be around.

Find The Optimistic Decision Makers—Become One

Try to be part of meetings with a decision-maker who radiates hope, promise and enthusiasm. If you can't work on his technical project, find a way to be on his soccer team or a task force of some kind. My best friends are those whom I've met in the interest of a project bigger than both of us. The energy expended when you have mutual goals is engaging and exciting.

How can you get close to that manager of International Marketing—four levels above you and out of the country most of the time? Read your organizational newsletter, talk to personnel, or just write your idol a letter. Tell him or her that you admire the work and style in which he or she produces. Tell that person you want to be involved some way, some day. Just plant the seed.

Without sounding too grandiose, my experience in the last ten years is that every time I do a major address or a training, someone comes up to me or writes to me that he or she would like to work with me in some way. My ego enjoys this. Tell me the person who does not feel good about getting positive feedback.

I also have people who tell me I'm not okay. I'm too loud, too emotional, not rational enough, repeat myself (you may notice this). I just don't fit with some people. It still hurts though. We human beings prefer to be loved or approved of by almost everyone with whom we come in contact.

But the person who can find a creative way to engage me, no matter how busy I am or how many requests I have, will tweak an interest and motivate me to try to set up something.

Be creative. I was giving a talk on **Persuasive Skills for the Technical Professional**, and somehow I mentioned how persuasive my new Miniature Schnauzer was. I also complained about her barking. Later I received in the mail, the book, *Why Dogs Bark*. This marvelous book by the author of the *Naked Ape,* Desmond Morris, tickled me so and was so informative, that, naturally, I had to contact the person who sent it to me and to give him some of my time.

When I talk about needing to lose weight and my walking routine, people call to ask if they can walk with me one morning while they pick my brain. Or they ask to take me to a new low-fat restaurant. I'm easy. Find out what vulnerable places your proposed mentor might have, and use them.

Now, you're saying that this sounds manipulative. If you are getting what you want, and the other person agrees to get what you have to offer to them, you are making a deal. Optimists know that making a win-win deal is the highest form of interaction. We do this successfully when we make love, co-chair a meeting, get a haircut, or introduce something to a person that he didn't even know he needed. I needed that dog book!

Becoming an optimistic decision-maker starts with small things. I was having lunch with the Senior Editor of *Inc. Magazine* a few years ago. He was interviewing me for a feature on 120 successful entrepreneurs that year. He interviewed from Iococca down to me.

We met in the posh, ever-so optimistic, Lion and Compass, owned by the ever-so optimistic Nolan Bushnell. The waiter brought us the optimistic menu. You know: 'Salmon with Drizzled Lemon Cream Sauce,' or 'Primo Baked Alaska' or 'Vine-Ripened Miniature Scarlet Tomatoes.'

I asked Curtis Hartman what quality all of the entrepreneurs he'd interviewed had in common. He did not hesitate, except that the waiter was now looking down at us. The editor replied, "they were all rapid decision-makers!"

As the waiter bowed to me, I rapidly made the decision: 'Delicate Scampi with Southern Spanish Amber Sauce!'

It's hard to make high-odds decisions. The Scampi was Low-odds. Responsibility requires making decisions at all ends of the spectrum. Optimists know this and don't complain over it. Our *Far Side* man explains that "the secret to inner peace is a short attention span." Amen—

If you feel a little uneasy with your role as an optimist, at first you may need to 'act as if.' Try the sounds of an optimist.

Optimists Say:

- ▲ can
- ▲ will
- ▲ want to
- ▲ yes!

They Don't Qualify With:

- ▲ probably
- ▲ maybe
- ▲ sometimes
- ▲ almost

Optimists sound definite, confident, at ease with a decision. I've learned that people who sweat every decision are simply afraid of making the **wrong one.** Someone must have convinced you that you were not good at decisions. Or you had parents who knew that there was only one right way to do things. Heaven help you.

Assume there are no wrong decisions. Just longer ones, or more circuitous ones, or more elaborate ones.

The pessimist may be right, but the Optimist will enjoy the ride!

Chapter 7

Detours, Rest Periods And Dormant Periods

Take A Break Or No Sex Life

Optimistic Organizations believe in breaks. They teach relief periods, coach over-workers how to balance their lives, and insist on changing the pace for employees who find themselves in a maze.

Science has taught us a lot about mazes. Those poor little rats don't even want to have a sex life if they are faced with constant maze frustration without a coffee break. Relief from any frustration, even tiny relief periods, seem to make the difference.

These same little rats, in psychological learning study laboratories, eventually give up food, water and social interaction. Many employees do the same. They end up in a corner facing the inevitable work load, without interest in luncheons, meetings, parties or any kind of a relationship life. Organizations tend to sponsor and reinforce this workaholic for the early periods in his tenure.

The poor employee usually can't objectively see when he is crossing the line from being a dedicated and brilliant employee to the one destined for stress management counseling. The narrowed approach, in any good cause or exciting project, without the break, can deteriorate the body and the soul.

Organizations that know the importance of change in routine, insist that their employees consider using the spas, the wellness clinics, the social breaks or the gyms, or at the least, some kind of outside activities. Apple Computer allows employees to swap snow cabin listings and softball team recruiting. They encourage a life after and during Apple. John Sculley's famous jogs were to encourage others to 'think physical fitness.'

If your organization doesn't foster relief, you, the reader, may be able teach how important rest periods can be. Bread alone is ultimately hard to digest. Teach this. You can do this by shaping your organization's behavior, slowly and scientifically.

Whenever there is anything company sponsored which you think offers a balanced life style, write to the President, your office newsletter, even your local newspaper. Do it in your electronic link, or just keep talking about it. Encourage policy, reward others who encourage positive policy. Sabbaticals are a way of life for many Silicon Valley companies. Unfortunately, in economic downturns, sabbaticals are among the first to go.

Good companies, however, simply postpone, knowing what a morale builder that ultimate vacation will be. If cash flow is poor, optimistic companies inform their people so they know exactly what is going on, and they can feel that their sabbatical postponement may be part of the solution, not the problem. In highly optimistic organizations, every member is part of the business decision and knows exactly why policy may be affecting his or her life.

Your organization may be a little slow about positive moves and executive decision communications. You may say it is too little, too late, or that there is much more to do. You are right. But appreciate the small steps and keep shaping change. Optimists believe that it is never too late. They translate that sometimes a long wait prepares one to appreciate a positive change. They may believe that the multi-married person was having to test out a few theories before he could make the right choices.

For yourself, learn to take small breaks. A five minute relaxation in which you assure yourself that you are going to feel more peaceful the rest of the day, works. The pessimist is all too eager to believe that five minutes is never enough.

The thirsty man who is parched may need to believe that the first few drops can save his life, and that there will be more as needed. If he is so busy worrying that these drops aren't going to be enough, or not coming fast enough, he will be using up the little energy he has left to worry about what could happen instead of appreciating what is happening—drops of water.

Optimists believe in the theory of abundance. They know there will be more. They believe they deserve more. They also know that taking a rest from a frustrating or wearying cause is medicine. They take the rest as preventive medicine.

The Dynamite Quarter

"This is our bad quarter, folks. The next one will be dynamite!"

We have hundreds of years of stock market rises and fall to convince us that what goes up usually goes down. Hills and valleys occur. Our heart beats with highs and lows. Biorhythms swing on cycles of 28 days and longer periods of time. The pendulum goes back and forth. Circadian rhythms manage and torment us.

Enduring organizations always capitalize on the down time. "This gives us an opportunity to restructure our accounting, or our work force, or our management style, or our customer base, or our landscaping!"

A bad quarter is only a precursor to a good quarter. We know that we wouldn't like chocolate mousse every night. It would get boring. I learned that on a cruise. After ten days, I longed for a plain old Oreo cookie.

If next quarter is not dynamite, you will have to take the opportunity to say that you may have needed two quarters, not one, to reorganize. Optimists capitulate. They are not afraid of it.

Detours Need A Life Of Their Own

Optimists believe they can make a wrong turn. If they do, they enjoy the ride and try to learn something from it. Leaders of good organizations are not afraid to respond:

"The journey into silicon micro mattresses was our focus for a long time last year. We learned a lot from that excursion."

Good companies believe that R&D really **does** mean **research** *and development.* They don't expect that the end result is always development. They know that research may end up with nothing substantial. They expect some backsliding and some economic stress. The price for a wrong turn can be built in, or it can be justified later. But it must be **justified.**

Space Travel Will Cure the Common Cold, Eventually. . . .
In the meantime, the space program has produced thousands of new products, a wide data base of information and a whole new way of approaching bio-technology. Eventually it will answer the common cold, optimists think. They also think that during the waiting period, the work accomplished was incredible. No small significance from the project was the morale boost to America. The space program created visionary thinking which has captured our hearts and our imaginations. This vision is also a product.

If your organization or your boss is on a detour for which you do not approve, relax. It will not do you any good to pout and complain. Make your arguments and then proceed as a team player toward the expressed goals.

Don't bother with "I told you so" either. This is a waste of time. The reminder will only produce the other's rationale for bad decisions, and will never grant you the satisfaction you desire. People lose their jobs over bad-mouthing the boss's projects. Others become outcasts when the majority of the organization is looking in one direction and the dissenters are looking in the other.

Being right is not as good as being in a relationship. Being right can be a lonely position.

Don't Rush, Resist Or Regret

If you are on a personal detour, try to take a look at the daisies on the trip. Holding tightly to old ways or courses you wish you were charting, can prevent you from seeing what is at hand. Perhaps this rest period or your own burn-out isn't in your big scheme of things. Maybe this project is beneath you or is not on your priority list. The belief that serendipity events can produce objectives not clearly mapped, is a comfortable way of being lost.

I was driving with my colleague to a speech I was to give within thirty minutes. We found ourselves hopelessly lost. It was raining. My colleague was screaming that we should have left earlier because of the rain. She was angry with herself for not getting better directions, and with me for being such an unconscious driver. The map was at the office and the car phone was being repaired. I stopped the car.

Then I proclaimed that I wanted to have a happy and peaceful afternoon, preferably with her. If she couldn't handle the mess we were in, I would find her a cab. But I wanted to try to use the time alone together, just to enjoy each other and drive around every street in the vicinity until we located the mystery spot. She promised to relax.

When I ended up in a dead end wrecking yard dirt road, she finally started to laugh. "Good, now we must be having fun," I chortled.

Eventually we got there. We were late. The organization shifted their schedule some. They made do. On the trip there, though, we finally decided to relax, no matter how long the trip would take. My staff member and I had a meaningful conversation. I learned new things about her college life. I shared my fear of premature death in family members. We even started some business plan work which was immensely creative for our company.

Resisting change or someone else's presumed bad ideas is wasteful. Let people catch up with your process. It's one thing to be such an advanced thinker that nobody is ever with you, but it is quite another to believe that they can never catch up. Learn to campaign for your ideas, projects or desires. And then learn to discipline yourself to shut up and wait for others to catch up!

Regretting is also wasteful. "If only" and "What if" are statements for losers who live in the future or the past. Optimists stay in the present. They enjoy it. This is the only moment you've got. Cherish it. Don't spend it on criticizing your past behaviors. Of course, learn from them, but don't spend so much energy on what didn't go right.

Dormancy Can Produce Fruit Salad—Unless You Cut Down The Tree

The dark winter trees are dreary and old looking. The limbs look frail or brittle or delicate. It is a barren sight.

In a few months, those same trees will begin to sprout some exquisite, beautiful, fragrant pink or white blossoms. Out of the cold, brown, dead looking leaves will come delicate flowers. The fresh green leaves will also appear.

And in a few months we will see the replacement for the blossom. A juicy and gorgeous peach or an apricot or a cherry may be the result. Out of that brown tree will appear this luscious piece of fruit.

Without the rest and dormancy period, the fruit will never appear. Without your own dormancy period, you may never produce again. So when you feel the despair of a quiet and non-fruitful period, relax with it. Believe this is the precursor to your own fruitful period.

Don't rush yourself or others or your organization out of dormancy. Holding tightly, or holding your breath, will not provide the oxygen for the growth. Start breathing again. Don't scare yourself. Allow for the quiet or unproductive time. Your fruitful time is in the next season.

When you believe in cultivation, fertilization, watering—not just the harvesting—you will be able to enjoy your full life. Planting seeds for yourself can be satisfying, but only if you believe that some of those seeds will thrive. Watering and fertilizing has to feel worthwhile. You need to believe that you are adding to the plant; that you are making a difference, even if you have no way of measuring this difference at this moment in time.

Don't cut down the tree before it blooms. Give yourself a little time before you cut yourself down. Consider your last three years. What has been going on for you? Did you really need a little break in creativity, productivity?

Ask For A Solution For Every Complaint

When you learn and when you teach the notion that for every problem, there is a solution, you can begin to show and feel trust. Some of the solutions will be off the wall; not valid or helpful, but some will make a difference. The act of presenting the solution or the option is the state of optimism.

- ▲ "This might work."
- ▲ "Perhaps we can."
- ▲ "I might have a way."
- ▲ "This could do the job."
- ▲ "Why don't we?"

These are all magical sentences which create optimism, power and hope.

Chapter 8

Maintain Optimism
In The Face Of Trouble

The 'Hardy Factor'

The 'hardy factor' is a measure of your resilience. If you bounce back, do not become too defeated too quickly, look for the positive way out, you are expressing hardiness. Every organization needs hardy folks who are not easily discouraged.

Optimists do not take criticism as deadly—but as feedback. They do not fall over from an ego push. They may bend with the wind, feel fragile some of the time, but they do not break.

The hardy boss, employee, love, mate, parent or child will take in data from others without necessarily believing that the data may be completely accurate.

Optimists bounce. They are prepared for bad times. And they prepare themselves to cope.

Foolish people believe that life should be easy. Then they are very disappointed when it is not. Smart people know that life will not be easy and they simply prepare to cope when it is not.

When looking for new teammates, employees or partners, ask how they handled adversity. Everyone handles success fairly well. We all do okay when things are easy. But find out what they did when the company downsized, or their mate left them, or the organization chose another president over them.

Ask the questions, "What would you do if you are assigned a poor manager?" If they quickly respond by suggesting they would ask for a transfer, stop the interview.

The answer you want is, "I would work to try to negotiate change with my manager. In the last result, I would try to coach my manager into different behavior. Or I would engage others to help me to coach change from him."

The Team Approach

Optimistic Organizations know that teams must work. They also expect that whenever you have two people on one task, you double the opportunity for misunderstandings and misgivings.

Henri Fayl, the great French Industrial Engineer, calculated that whenever you have ten subordinates working together, you have 6133 opportunities for conflict. Just think of the possibilities if you have a few more than ten in a team. The combination of people who can strike alliances and who can team up to discourage each other are so incredibly large that it is amazing we get anything accomplished in teams.

That is why team leadership is so important. It is also why team role assignments and division of labor can be so vital. Optimistic Teams, motivated and encouraged by good leadership can do anything. There will always be the individual contributor or the lone wolf or the 'doubting Thomas' on a team.

Good teams coach optimism by example and shaping behavior. They don't get discouraged with a sour grape. They expect a few. Plan for them. Cope with them. They don't complain or cry about the man or woman who has not learned to be a team player. Positive teams know that the odds produce the complete spectrum of personality types. You're lucky if you have a great team without a lot of training and encouragement. And you are lucky if the team **remains** great without training and encouragement.

In the era of specialization, one specialist sometimes must team up with another. At other times, the whole organization must collaborate with manufacturing and marketing and sales departments. Do teams work? Why is it sometimes so hard?

Some People Are Trained By The Scientific Method

Some people just naturally check for flaws first. They are taught to consider the problems before accepting the possibilities. These patterns conflict with basic 'group think.' It is hard to stay open to the sales director's ideas without considering the improbabilities of his suggestions. The brain-storming theory of listening without judging is a forum for cognitive dissonance. We want to listen, but we also want to object!

Fix It By:

Learn the value of brain-storming and conceptual block-busting with courses and books which insist that group think is ultimately more productive than uni-think. Of course there are times which call for complete one dimensional concentration, but stifle your reflex reaction to this comfortable mode, for the 'good of the order.'

Many Of Us Think In Uni-Focus

This unilateral focus provides for the ultimate concentration on creative tasks, without the distraction of other dimensional pulls. The price, though, is missing out on some early strategic 'big picture' thinking. The rush to the problem at hand, especially if it is technically provocative, screens out people and other ideas if you concentrate on a single issue.

Fix It By:

Train yourself to hold back. Don't zero in on one aspect of the problem. Leave it open. This is crucial in the planning stages of any project. Re-program yourself with self talk. Believe that you can use more left brain or right brain, adding the other dimension. Practice driving and talking, being on a serious phone call and adding columns, or deliberating on two or more projects on at time.

Some Team Members Are Inherently More Introspective and Introverted.

Many of your colleagues are introverts—that is, they process problems internally before they collaborate. Teambuilding may actually be frightening. People who are not prone toward inter-action and high communication skills increase that 'contagious reserve' which can prevent group interaction. Like a convention of shy people, not much happens. Everyone waits for the 'stimu-lator' to start the action!

Fix It By:

Training and group supervision in communication. Practice interaction with others on a regular basis. Practice the dreaded 'small talk.' Fear of rejection, inability to 'mix-it-up,' and lack of experience in being vulnerable, all prohibit interactive behaviors. The introvert processes events, problems and people internally, while the extrovert translates and works on the problem with others, out loud. A compromise so others can know how you think and draw conclusions is vital to your team. Talk out your problems. Announce your own processing style. It won't hurt as much as being misunderstood.

Interdependency Not Coached

We tend to look upon dependence as weakness. Unable to distinguish what alternating dependency would look like, the 'do-it-yourselfer' has difficulty believing or relying on the expertise of others. This is why so many independents do their own taxes, (even if they don't 'do' them, they prepare them initially and expect the tax consultant to simply look for flaws in logic or math.) Teams turn sour when alternating dependency doesn't happen. If leadership doesn't shift some, or if team members can't assign individualized roles to each other, based on strength, the team will not develop.

Fix It By:

'Anchor' onto past events in which you have felt like a team player. If none come to mind, explore your family roles with siblings or the way your parents showed co-equal team roles. If no insight occurs, take classes in team building. Read *Styles of Thinking,* by Bob Bramson, and push yourself into collaborative projects, some non-threatening if possible, just for practice! Learn to trust and appreciate the skills of your team mates.

Being On a Team Means Accepting Rational and Irrational Conclusions

This hurts. It is hard to close your eyes and push forward in a collaborative effort when you believe others are proceeding from faulty concepts. Instead of 'pitching' the team in your theory's direction, you may sit back and passive-aggressively not cooperate.

Fix It By:

Appreciate complementary working relationships. In other arenas, your mate or support personnel may actually be more emotionally sensitive than you are, and this works. Learn the language of 'internal response systems' (feelings!) Start with: "I don't know what to say right now; I'm certain there are appropriate responses, but I'm a little dumbfounded." In a team-building situation, it's okay to say: "I want to be a teammate with you, but I'm not too good at this. My intentions are honorable, though, so help me out when you see I'm slipping."

I believe in the systems approach to problem-solving. Optimists are also good students who learn to adjust personalities, patterns and behaviors when it will advance the company or them selves. Teams work when individuals want to work together. Individuals need to give up control, shift power, and sometimes take responsibility for the whole darned team. Push your own ideas, pitch for what you want. We know that it is easier to do it yourself. But only in the short term. In the meantime, try for some consensus thinking. It sometimes takes longer. It sometimes works.

The Boy And Girl Scouts Of America: Be Prepared

Every girl and boy scout is taught to be prepared, for emergencies, for assisting others, for aiding their country, for coping with crisis. They are taught the rudiments of self preservation; they are also taught the **attitude of self preservation,** with good spirit, good humor, good service, good listening. Peter Druker called the Girls Scouts the best managed organization in America.

Does your organization believe in prevention work? Are you or your company proactive? Do you think ahead, planning for interventions when things get shaky, looking for dilemmas to fix, for competition to challenge you, and for planning for the next crisis. I'm not talking about being a 'crisis junkie.' These folks are always looking for trouble; often falling in the middle of it. They don't seem content until erratic behavior or trauma is unwrapping the organization. They are dangerous.

Crisis junkies are interesting to be around. They are seductive too, because they seem so darned interested in fixing the dilemma. The problem is that their hysterical nature actually causes the dilemma in the first place. Now, we used to associate 'hysterical' with women. I have worked in groups where the men provoked riots. Watch for the types who never seem to leave well enough alone. In the beginning, they seem vital to the organization. In the end, they seem old. Their tantrums are old too.

Teach every one you know that "this may be as good as it gets" so you can all prepare for the drought or the floods or the storm or the stillness. Farmers learned to store away goods in the basement for the next bad winter. Companies learn to prepare for emergency funds. Cities budget for contingency funds. Educational foundations lay away pockets in general funds. Individuals plan for IRAs and other prevention plans.

Preventive attitudes are more ambiguous and subtle. The message of hope and trust in others may be quiet, but they are powerful and important messages that can change directions for an entire organization. Teach your colleagues that their preventive positive attitudes can subvert tragedy. Their preventive positive attitudes can divert rebellions. Their proactive positive attitudes can save organizations.

Happiness is a Choice, Robert Fritz proclaims in his book by that name. Present a choice to every member of your team. Sometimes people are so paralyzed that they can't think of options. As a counselor and a consultant in our **Distinguished Employee and Executive Program**, we know the employee will sometimes come in dry, devoid of options. Our job is to juice up the choices with lots of ways to get out of the current dilemma. Presenting new options is a psychological life-saver.

Those little 'smile' stickers are out of vogue. So are the 'I love my Irish Setter' posters. Without the stickers and other reminders, how does an organization set the scene for optimism? By you, this reader. By your enthusiasm, by your campaigns for rewarding positive thinking and preventive action. By noting and noticing and notarizing positive attitudes. By enormous hand shakes and 'thank yous' and promotions and prizes to those who shape the changes in others!

Resilient Organizations Change, Merge, Acquire, Sell Or Sustain

Expect change. When Apple Computer encouraged Steve Job's departure, the company experienced all the trauma of a parent abandoning a family. In this case, though, the parent didn't choose to abandon, so maybe it was more like a kidnapping. In any case, the kids were without the father they had learned to accept. A concept, a character, a spirit was lifted from the organization. The replacement man, John Sculley, was as different as he could be. Jobs and Sculley had many common goals, but their working styles and life experiences had been drawn from two diametrically different vantage points.

There was an emotional shudder that rocked the company which had never imagined life without Steven Jobs. The resilient Apple lived through the transition. Sculley helped. Others helped. The stability of the old guard helped too. The change of command was quick and dramatic. And Jobs started a new company, NeXT.

In this case, the tremendous and accepted Apple products encouraged optimism among the troops. The scintillating company image propelled the employees through the hard times. The transition team bridged the emotional gaps in management. They made it.

This change prepared Apple Computer for the many changes to come. There may have been too many re-organizations, but each one was presented with vigor and a 'this will help' attitude.

The passion of a resilient organization will get you through hard times. Recently some of our most famous department stores seem to be giving up, breaking up. Resilience will sustain those who make it.

I am more impressed with stores like Montgomery Ward and J. C. Penny because they have had to make multiple marketing switches over the last twenty years. Each company nearly gave up, and in the nick of time, it would seem to outsiders, they pulled out some strategic decision to be different, and the company survived. The prognosis for an organization which has had some dips and dives and shows signs of strength in spite of them: Excellent.

Silicon Valley electronic companies have probably produced more mergers and acquisitions and sales and endings of organizations per square foot than anywhere in the world. Yet, the stable organizations around the area, IEEE, American Electronics Association and the Manufacturing Group sustained momentum for the morale of the community.

In spite of high profile blendings of companies, many have seemed to thrive in the chaos, and some have remained untouched by the chaos. Corporate CEOs and CFOs have traveled from Measurex to Rolm to IBM to DEC to Silicon Graphics. Hewlett Packard birthed thousands of managers who eventually moved to start-ups or middle-ups or other forms of innovative ways of being in business.

Good Old Companies Never Die

They live on in the hearts of those who nurtured and grew them. Four Phase, Dysan and Intel founders still pepper the current sphere of influence with their former stars. Employee groups move in mass together, usually arriving in single file, recruited by an age-old colleague, but ultimately all meeting together in new company forms. They take what was good from the old company, use what still works, and if they are mature, they look back with fondness about the experiments which now serve them.

Dad Was A Pessimist

What if you grew up or were mentored by pessimists? Many of us were. Your parents or grandparents were immigrants and did not trust the new system, culture or government. Their fears and helplessness penetrated your emotional pores. Your reflex action, may, then, be to jump when something seems authoritarian or out of your control.

Your father may have declared bankruptcy in your last year in graduate school. He may never have recovered. Does it take its toll on you? Of course. Financial downturns may invoke primal pains, with triggers from your broken father as well as your own sense of loss.

To change that script, first acknowledge how deeply you have been penetrated by the fear and anxiety. Then accept yourself as having that handicap. If you push it away, deny that you have ever been affected, or imagine that you have completely overcome your history, you may be fooling yourself, but, more fatally, you may be preventing yourself from giving up the script. It's hard to give up alcoholism or any other 'ism' if you do not believe it is an 'ism.' So look at your teachers, relatives, former mentors, the folks who instilled terror of risk, and allow that to have been part of your life.

Then accept yourself, like yourself, all right—love yourself, even though these old demons seem to appear out of nowhere. When someone says something to hurt my feelings, or especially when I have done something humiliating or stupid, it's important for me to accentuate my positive self. Ala Muriel James, who wrote *Born to Win,* and who has indelibly inspired me, we need this self talk when we feel misunderstood.

I need to say to myself, "Aw, Jeannie. It's okay. You didn't mean it, or you couldn't help it. You did the best you could." Sometimes that nurturing parent inside of me has to say, "They don't know what they are talking about. You really are a good kid, and what do they know?"

Men have an even harder time than women with nurturing themselves when they have been slighted.

If you've learned the scientific method: weigh all the circumstances, check all the possible misfires or reservations, and only then you can be easy on yourself. My CEO, a recovered aerospace engineer of many years, used to respond to my enthusiastic proposal, after looking over the brief, with "I don't see any reason why not."

This drove me crazy. The time he spent looking for flaws in the contract or inspecting for reservations, made me believe he really did not want to do it. The final "I don't see any reason why not" certainly turned me off. By then I had concluded a lot of reasons **why not**.

I taught Dick to be a little more enthusiastic at the beginning, and to hold the major assessment until after he had given me a tentative approval of the concept of the proposal. He taught me to be patient and wait for at least a cursory scanning for problems. And when he presents a job or proposal to me, I give him response in his form. I completely digest the document, in his deliberating way, before I say 'yes.' Then he can be sure of my 'yes.'

I also am married to a rational and careful man who would do much more preliminary work before he would make a positive remark. We have taught each other that if it is about my work, my mother, my brother, my special projects, he will respond as quickly as possible. If it is about his work, his brother, his special projects, I will research first and give an absolute 'yes,' and not the one that used to mean '**maybe**.'

We need the pessimistic reality checks. We need people who are cautious and not overly idealistic. Every organization needs that conservative influence to temper the ultra-optimist who is often just plain out of touch.

Dr. Seligman reminds us: "In some situations—the cockpit of an airliner, for example—what's needed is not an upbeat view, but a mercilessly realistic view."

When Crisis Knocks—Answer

The real optimist lives through crises. The dimension of that life, of course, depends on the kind of crisis. If you have a career crisis, a layoff, a termination, a demotion, you can enthusiastically answer that knock on the door. You have a lot to learn about you. This is the time to learn it. You are listening very carefully now, I notice.

Too many people ignore the knock. They hear it faintly, and pretend to themselves that it must be for someone else. That is why they are surprised when the termination notice appears and they are unprepared for it. Some people actually have been given a year's severance pay, but won't consider looking for another job until the time is out. They haven't enjoyed the vacation either. They simply did not want to face the real facts.

Personal crises happen to positive people too. Scott Neely, a man I admire, lost a son in a tragic way. He lost his *only* son. The family was devastated. Scott used the loss to inspire him to encourage men to express their feelings, to be open to vulnerability. Scott has since saved the emotional lives of countless people he touches.

Judith Briles, author of eight books, and my friend, also lost a son in a tragic way. She now uses the tragedy to help others, to understand herself, to express her own pain in many arenas. Judith suffered. Now Judith serves. She stayed open.

Just as we do selective listening in business, people close down personally too. People do not want all the facts in relationships too. In my counseling practice, I have had 500 couples in which one mate is completely surprised and flabbergasted that the other mate wants to leave the marriage. Who was not listening? Now, I know, from much history, that mates who want to leave, or who are having affairs, are often reluctant to clue the other partner in too soon. Isn't this sad?

But the reluctant party (the one who does not want the separation) needs to look at his part in the deception. Could he have read some signs if he was willing to?

The first symptom of marital or career distress is when the other person begins to ignore you, won't meet your eyes, misses meetings together, and seems indifferent. If you are being left off memos, meetings or project planning, get a clue! You have lost communication with the person who most affects you. Then, knowing that, you still may feel afraid to make the move toward communication.

The optimist will step up and say, "Dave, we seem to be having a problem. You are not talking to me. You are not including me in the project meetings, and you seem to ignore me completely. What is going on?" This is a door opener.

In a relationship, Marvin needs to say to his wife, Jane: "Honey, something must be happening with you about me. I am not sensing your interest in getting together with me. You are not complaining, but you are also not saying anything to me. I feel the drift. I'd like a chance to know what is going on before it is too late." Wow—another opportunity seized!

I'm not saying it is easy to look at problems. If you are in crisis, what is your behavioral style. Do you?

▲   hide away
▲   get offensive
▲   get demanding
▲   distract yourself
▲   pretend it isn't happening
▲   up the good behavior

Frankly, upping the good behavior won't help either. You need to find out exactly what is going wrong. Sending the roses, getting to work on time at last, may not help. Get the information. The right information.

The optimist, of course, will believe in second chances, or will believe that he can persuade the disenchanted to take another look. The ultimate optimist will do his best, and then move on if he must.

In organizations, optimism requires tactics for crisis. Talk to your team ahead of time. Things happen. Plan on them. Plan on talking about your individual crisis styles too. We did a lot of counseling in companies during the California earthquake of

1989, and we learned a lot about the way people cope. Find out about your colleagues, before you have to be surprised.

Our Center served as the counseling center for families of the Desert Storm War in 1991. Four hundred families touched us, and vice-versa. We learned in this arena, again, how predominant *"learned helplessness"* was in those most impotent to cope. Sometimes this appeared in the service men and women overseas, too. The courageous and positive loved ones correlated with low morale service people.

Teach Power Talk

When optimistic organizations meet, there will be power talk. It sounds like this:

- ▲ We can do it.
- ▲ Let's start.
- ▲ Let us at them.
- ▲ We've got enough.
- ▲ We're good enough.
- ▲ There is time enough.
- ▲ They are lucky to have us.
- ▲ What a team!

The eighty-five year old noted sociologist, Ashley Montague, was addressing 7000 counselors in Phoenix in our conference in 1989. He claimed that the "Scientist believes in **certainty without proof** and that other people believe in **proof without certainty**."

Powerful teams and organizations and people try to look at certainty from both directions. A pragmatic manager knows how high he can jump. A successful president knows how much he can risk. A good mate knows how much he can take. You know how much balance you need in your life to feel confident and powerful.

You know, don't you, that we are talking of **power to** and not **power over.** I believe that powerful people are willing to take responsibility for people. Sometimes that is confused with power over. Helpless people are afraid to take responsibility for themselves, no less others.

I believe that powerful people are aware of their limitations and are willing to set boundaries. They are willing to reach out and make a difference. They rarely worry about humiliation, embarrassment or trying too hard. They feel good in the attempt. They don't expect perfection from themselves. They don't die if they fail. They look forward. "Give me another try," the ultimate optimist begs.

Start asking for more. Stop worrying about your imperfections and your learning disabilities. Congressmen have them. Presidents have them. Your boss has them. We all have them.

Power talk is not making excuses. It assumes excuses. It is volunteering, taking the risk, being first, touching the untouchable, and saying the unspeakable—with sensitivity.

"Executive team members, I believe we have a problem we have not been facing. The quality of our product is slipping to dangerous and expensive levels. I have some suggestions to fix it. I know this takes daring and guts. I've got some. Maybe enough for a few of you. And to the rest of you: I urge you to fix this problem with me. We can do it together."

Powerful positive talkers rarely qualify, discount, deny, equivocate. This confidence invokes confidence. They know others want you to be right, to inform, to entertain, to motivate, to feed them. The optimist does not expect others to sabotage, to poke holes, to wish failure, to expect to be bored or manipulated.

Our basic human nature is to want to trust each other. Watch a new baby who feels safe and warm and secure. Watch a confident little three year old who is used to smiles and warmth wherever he goes. Only when he grows up, to be measured, tested, humiliated, shamed, will he feel concern about others.

Optimists trust others. Start doing this. It's easier. It's cleaner. It's faster. And you can learn it!

About GLC

Growth & Leadership Center (GLC) was established in 1980. Its vision:

> *GLC will stimulate the Good Life for everyone who walks in the door, and will provide the Good Life for all GLC staff.*

The *Distinguished Employee Program* offers high potential executives or employees consulting until they meet corporate and their own objectives.

With 200 companies, from IBM to GM to Apple, GLC has trained, consulted and counseled thousands. With leading edge corporate psychology, a staff of 20 from the business and psychological world, GLC stimulates organizations to get, grow and keep optimism.

Hollands, President, has presented in every corporate forum and conference in the country, from IEEE to MIT, Minnesota, to the high profile winners in Silicon Valley.

Growth & Leadership Center
1451 Grant Rd, Ste. 102
Mountain View, CA 94040
(415) 966-1144

Index